Two Years in Fiji

Two Years in Fiji

A FAMILY ADVENTURE

Fiona Mullany

Published privately in 2021 by Fiona Mullany
Edited by Tracey Hawthorne
Designed by Triple M Design
Set in 10.5/18pt Georgia

To my beautiful family,
for their continuous support.

Fiji Islands

Yasawa Group

Vanua Levu

Taveuni

Koro

Ovalav

Viti Levu

Ngau

Vatulele

Moala Group

Kadavu

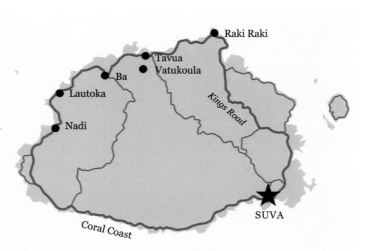

Raki Raki

Tavua
Vatukoula

Ba

Kings Road

Lautoka

Nadi

SUVA

Coral Coast

Vitu Levu

Contents

Prologue

‡

Sitting in the classroom, we could hear a rhythmic pounding sound, which the teacher explained was the school caretaker getting the kava ready for us by pounding and crushing the roots of the *Piper methysticum* plant.

When the caretaker brought the powder into the classroom, the teacher indicated that we should all sit cross-legged on the mat around the big wooden kava ceremonial bowl. The teacher added water to the brownish powder, mixing it until it resembled dirty water. I must say, it didn't look very appetising. My friend Judy and I, and the other three students, were exchanging some nervous glances.

I was concerned about the water the teacher was using, which I was pretty sure was just plain river water. We'd all been strongly advised not to drink the tap water and told to use bottled water even to brush our teeth. And it quickly became apparent that all six of us would be drinking from the same container, which was half a coconut shell.

I decided to throw caution to the wind, whispered to myself, 'Que sera, sera,' and committed myself to enjoying the experience.

The teacher clapped once, filled the coconut shell with the

dirty-looking mixture, yelled 'Bula!' (Cheers!), then drank it down in one gulp. When he finished, he placed the cup back in the bowl and clapped three times while saying 'Maca' (Thank you). He then turned to the person on his right, which was a very sceptical Judy, and asked her if she'd like a 'high tide' (a full container) or a 'low tide' (half a container).

She opted for a low tide, took the cup, clapped, said 'Bula!' then closed her eyes and went for it. She did make a bit of a face but finished off by clapping three times and yelling 'Maca!'

My turn was next. Judy whispered, 'Gulp it down as quick as you can or you won't finish it.'

I asked for a low tide and completed the ritual. The drink tasted like mud, but what really shocked me was the tingling feeling in my mouth. It also seemed to suck all the saliva out, but it did leave me with a sense of calm, relaxation and general lethargy.

We kept going until the bowl was completely empty and everyone was feeling very mellow.

Kava (or yaqona) is Fiji's national drink, made from the pulverised root of a member of the pepper family and believed to have medicinal qualities. Legend has it that the kava ceremony came from Tonga, where the plant sprang from the grave of a Tongan princess who'd died of a broken heart.

But what was I, a French-born, English-speaking mother of two, wife of a mining engineer, doing in Fiji, drinking kava with an eclectic group of adult students from all corners of the world?

Unexpected beginnings

There's nothing quite like a phone ringing in the small hours of the morning to get the heart pumping. So when we were torn from sleep that morning at 3 by the sound, my nerves continued jangling long after my husband, Ivan, had answered it and reassured me that it wasn't bad news.

That pre-dawn phonecall did, however, herald a huge change for our family – the beginning of an extraordinary adventure.

The caller was a colleague of Ivan's, telling him of a fabulous job opportunity. The reason he'd called at 3am was that he was in Fiji, and he hadn't factored in the ten-hour time difference between there and us in France.

Ivan, a metallurgist, was in the market for employment, if not immediately then certainly at some stage in the nearish future. At the time of the call, he was working on Salsigne Gold Mine, which had resources to last one or two more years, after which he was going to be out of work.

The prospective position was with the Emperor Gold Mine in Fiji, a 300-island archipelago in the southern Pacific Ocean about 2 000 kilometres northeast of New Zealand. Ivan was very familiar with the company, as it was where he'd been working before coming to France two years before, to work at Salsigne. A graduate of Murdoch University in Perth, Australia, Ivan had found Fiji to be a huge learning curve: he'd got to work with some highly experienced mining engineers and metallurgists whom he credits for mentoring him and teaching him invaluable lessons both personally and professionally.

'I think we should go,' my husband said, as we sat in bed discussing it at 4 in the morning. 'It'll be such an amazing place for our family.' He went to fetch some photo albums, full of happy snaps he'd taken during his previous time in Fiji, and dumped them in my lap. 'Look through these and tell me what you think later today.'

With that, he rolled over and was snoring in no time.

But it was the end of my night.

▲ ▲ ▲

The beautiful historic town of Carcassonne in the south of France is nestled among vineyards and mountains. Renowned for its medieval citadel, most of its construction dates back to the 12th and 13th centuries, with some walls as old as the Roman times. (Some might recognise the Cité de Carcassonne as part of the backdrop for the 1991 movie *Robin Hood: Prince of Thieves* starring Kevin Costner.)

The whole area is just delightful: the landscape is very picturesque, the weather is amazing (hot in summer and mild in winter), the food is delicious (some of France's best-known dishes originate from this region) and the wine is abundant and very good.

This is where our hotel, Hotel Astoria, was located. It was a busy little place as we were lucky to be mentioned in many travel guides. Our reputation as an English-speaking establishment helped us to build a solid anglophone clientele, business people and holidaymakers alike.

My two young children grew up there; they thought it was perfectly normal to live in an oversized house with lots of strangers popping in for the night. Melina, my elder child, is a real chatterbox and loved helping me on reception, while her younger brother Mansell usually hung out in the kitchen hoping for a spare croissant or a hot chocolate.

In 1993, a small hundred-year-old goldmine located about eighteen kilometres north of Carcassonne was bought by an Australian company. They invested a huge amount of capital in the processing plant, and the engineers involved in this project, mostly Australians and Britons, stayed at our hotel for the eighteen months it took to complete the work. During this time a strong friendship formed between us all, and it was bittersweet to see them finishing up.

As a send-off for the old team and welcome party for the replacement one coming in to run the operations, we all gathered at a restaurant in the town. Everyone was eyeing out the two new kids on the block, Toni, an Australian, and Ivan, who'd come from the Fiji Islands.

Ivan sat next to me, and for the next few hours we chatted mostly to each other, completely ignoring the other people at the table. He was curious to know how I spoke English, and I wanted to know if he was really Fijian. He was easy to talk to and had a great sense of humour, and I loved the cheeky little twinkle in his eye. I found out we had a few things in common, not least our complicated backgrounds.

He was born in South Africa but emigrated with his family to Australia when he was 13, and considered himself Australian; and I explained how my parents and brothers were all English but that I was French, as my mom and dad had emigrated to France for my dad's work a few years before they'd had me. I was born in Paris and went to school in France.

I told Ivan about my father's accident when I was 16, by that stage living with him and my mother in Brussels. He had a fall down a flight of stairs and broke not only some vertebrae in his lower back but also his left femur. The accident left him with irreversible damage to his health, and a panel of doctors recommended he be put on disability pension. During the next eighteen months, while my parents' focus was entirely on getting my father out of his wheelchair and back on his feet, I was left to my own devices and ran somewhat wild.

When my parents decided to move full time to their holiday home in Spain, in the hopes that the warmer weather would help my father's recovery, I was happy to tag along. I enrolled in a language school where I learnt to speak Spanish and soon after fell in love with a Spaniard. He was a hotel receptionist by day and a singer, entertaining tourists in the evenings. By the time I was 22, we had two children, and although they were the best things that had ever happened to me, I did have a deep-seated sense of having lost my way somewhere.

Then my father had a stroke, and we all decided to move to

France, where the medical system could deal with his needs. We came up with a plan of buying a small hotel we could run together.

The business side of our plan worked well but, not too surprisingly, my marriage didn't, and the Spaniard returned to his home country, leaving my mother, my father and I to run the hotel – and that's what I was doing when I met Ivan.

▲ ▲ ▲

Although Ivan and I had a wonderful time together at the farewell dinner, life got busy for both of us and we didn't reconnect for many months. Then one evening, out of the blue, Ivan rang me to ask if I'd like to go with him to a village fete. These are very common all over France during the summer months. A village will hire a band, set up some chairs and tables in the town square, and people can enjoy a few drinks and a meal while listening or dancing to some live music. Mas Cabardes, where we were going, was renowned for its summer jazz festival.

It was a lovely warm night, and the music was wonderful – our love for jazz was another thing we had in common – although we didn't do much dancing, choosing instead to talk and get to know each other more.

And that was the beginning of our romance. The next dates were just as wonderful, and on the evenings we couldn't see each other due to work commitments, Ivan would still find a way to come by late at night, knocking on my window for a goodnight kiss.

Over the next few months, we took the kids with us on several outings. We went horse riding, to the beach and on picnics, and we explored an array of old ruins sprinkled around the country-side. It was a pleasure watching the three of them interact, despite the language barrier – my children spoke only French, and Ivan's French was very basic. But Ivan was a natural with the kids, and watching them chatting and laughing together made me fall even more in love with him. The four of us quickly became a true family, to the delight of my parents, who were glad to see their grand-children smiling and happy again.

Ivan and I got married in January 1996, two years after our first meeting. It was a beautiful winter's day, and the ceremony was in the town hall. His parents flew in from Perth. My witness was my very good friend Arnaud (also my hairdresser, our chauffeur, the MC and dance teacher) and Ivan's was his good friend Mike. My beautiful little flower girl was Melina. Mansell was too shy to take part but made an appearance for the photos.

Ivan was very concerned because his French was still quite limited and he was worried he wouldn't know when to say 'Oui' but I promised I'd nudge him when the time came. It all went off without a hitch. It was a perfect day.

*Ivan and I tied the knot on 20 January 1996. My dress was ivory with a
touch of burgundy, with the same colours and styles mirrored in
Ivan's, Melina's and Mansell's outfits.*

Heart-wrenching goodbyes

Ivan and I spent many, many hours discussing his job offer and the prospect of moving lock, stock and barrel to Fiji. The opportunity was a promotion for him, and now that he had an 'instant family' to take care of, the extra money would come in handy.

Together, we looked at options and alternatives, examining the positives, the negatives and everything in between.

For me, the big obstacle was leaving my family behind, and this weighed heavily on my mind. Over the next couple of months, I had numerous changes of heart, and once I even told Ivan to go without me. 'If you're not coming, I'm not going either,' he said, and I knew he meant it.

Finally, having made the decision to move, we had to tell my parents. I couldn't do it – my stomach was in a knot; I couldn't breathe and my heart was pounding. I let Ivan explain the situation.

My mum started crying and my dad, keeping a true English stiff upper lip, just closed his eyes, sighed heavily, and then started asking pertinent questions about medical insurance and accommodation. As a geography buff, he was also interested in knowing which island the mine was located on, how far it was to the nearest town or city, and what the infrastructure was like. 'You know the islands are prone to being hit by cyclones?' he said, concerned. Dear old Dad, always looking out for his daughter and grandkids.

I later discovered my mother had done something quite extraordinary: when I contacted my divorce lawyer to find out my rights and responsibilities involving emigrating with my children (I was allowed to take the children with me, he informed me), he mentioned that my mum had already contacted him to see if anything could be done to prevent me from taking the children to Fiji. Emotions were running high for all of us, and I couldn't hold it against her; I never told her I knew what she'd tried to do. The truth was, I felt guilty for the pain I was causing my dad and her: I owed them so much, and they had stuck by me through thick and thin.

The kids had also never known life without their Nana and Grandad. When a thunderstorm was brewing, Melina would run to my mum, as she knew her grandma would take her to a safe hiding place – my mum was almost as scared of storms as Melina. Mansell always sat on Grandad's lap in the hopes of hearing another story about his favourite teddy bear. My dad was a great storyteller – when I was a little girl, I would sometimes pretend to have nightmares and call out for him in the middle of the night, just to have him sit on my bed and transport me into a magical world.

And it wasn't like we were moving to another town or another European country; no, we were going to some obscure little island on the other side of the world.

Given the circumstances, my parents expressed their wish to retire, and said they didn't want to continue running the hotel on their own. Luckily a buyer was quickly found, so my transitioning out of the business was easier than I thought it would be.

Still, the next few weeks, as we prepared for the big move, were an emotional rollercoaster ride. All the travel books I picked up about the Fiji Islands (this was before the days of Google or TripAdvisor) showed friendly faces, pristine beaches and crystal-clear waters. I had a vision of dropping the kids off at school, then heading down to the beach with my straw hat, a book and a piña colada. Life would be so relaxing and splendid.

But there were devastating lows, too. Three weeks before our departure, my mum asked us to leave the hotel. She couldn't handle seeing her grandchildren every day knowing that soon they would no longer be in her life. Luckily, friends offered us their holiday home on the outskirts of Carcassonne for our remaining time.

My mom's and my relationship hit another low when I contacted her with a list of personal belongings that we needed to get from the hotel. She kindly agreed to have them delivered to us in the late afternoon, which suited me as I was out all day running last-minute errands. Words can't describe the shock I got when, turning onto the street, I saw all our precious belongings carelessly thrown onto the front lawn of our temporary accommodation. The children's beds, our clothes, computer and other personal effects had just been tossed there like rubbish. I found out later that Mum had recruited a friend of mine who owned a van (and who apparently also needed to vent his anger at my leaving) to help her carry out this ultimate theatrical gesture of discontent towards Ivan and me.

As the days went on, my resolve and determination started to weaken. As a last resort to try to get me to stay, my mum played on my father's failing health – he'd suffered a heart attack the previous year from which he'd not completely recovered – and a couple of times I broke down and told Ivan that he'd have to go without me. He could see the uncertainty I was going through and kept reassuring me that if I didn't want to go, he would stand by my side. His support meant everything to me.

What finally freed me was an unexpected call I got from my dad one morning. He asked me to meet him by the Canal du Midi – a marvellous piece of waterway engineering, linking the Atlantic to the Mediterranean via a number of locks, aqueducts, bridges and tunnels – and take a walk with him.

We met at his favourite spot, overlooking the Carcassonne locks. I ran into his arms, sobbing. 'Dad, I'm so sorry for the pain I'm putting you and Mum through,' I cried. 'I'm also distraught at the idea of leaving you. I can't handle it any more, so if you tell me to stay, I will.' I was a complete blubbering mess.

My dad pushed me away gently, holding me at arms' length and looking into my eyes. 'My darling girl,' he said. 'I've lived a wonderful life, made even more beautiful by you and your kids, and I thank you for that. Now it's time for you to go, to follow your husband. Don't worry about me or your mum; we'll be okay. You must go and live your life. I know you love us with all your heart, and that you'll come back to visit.' Then he hugged me tight.

I was thankful beyond words can express for his blessing. A huge weight was lifted off my shoulders. Our final goodbyes would still be difficult but, for now, my focus could be spent on the task ahead.

At the airport in Toulouse, France, in August 1996. Although I'm smiling on the outside, I was a jangle of nerves on the inside, full of trepidation about leaving behind everything and everyone familiar to me.

Arrival

Nadi is the major transport hub of Fiji and located on the main island of Viti Levu. That was where we touched down after a 36-hour journey, and where Brad was waiting to fetch us.

'The company has booked you into the Mocambo Hotel for two nights as a welcome gift,' he told us.

'That's very kind of them but I think I'd prefer to get to our new home and start settling in straight away,' I said.

The two men glanced at each other. It was an unspoken message that I didn't query at the time, but understood later when I finally saw our comfortable but basic abode, to enjoy the little luxuries that came our way. 'You know what, love?' Ivan said to me. 'I think it's a brilliant idea to spend some time getting over the jet lag down here in Nadi.' When he saw I was still hesitating, he quickly added, 'Plus, the kids will enjoy spending time in the pool.'

And he was right – we spent a heavenly two days lazing around the pool, drinking fruit punch and discovering some local dishes. My favourite was kokoda, a kind of ceviche made with coconut cream, giving it an amazing balance of acidity and richness.

But all good things come to an end, and soon it was time for us to hit the road towards our new life and temporary home – the housing manager had explained that the house they had in mind for us was still being renovated and would only be ready in a couple of months' time. We weren't bothered, as our furniture and most of our belongings were still on a ship somewhere on the Pacific Ocean.

An old beaten-up four-wheel-drive had been dropped off at the hotel: this would be our family car. We all piled in, along with our luggage, and set off north, up Kings Road, towards Vatukoula. The distance was only 96 kilometres, but it was a very hazardous drive and took a full two hours to complete.

We shared the road with pedestrians, cows, goats and horses, and quickly learnt that if you kept your hand on the horn, you'd apparently be safe, even while overtaking on a blind bend or just stopping in the middle of the road to pick up or drop off people and goods.

I covered my eyes with my hands, and Ivan laughed. 'Wait till you see what night driving is like,' he said. 'The understanding is that having your lights on will drain the battery, so most people drive in complete darkness.'

Not totally sure if he was pulling my leg, I laughed along with him and decided to concentrate more on my surroundings and let him worry about the road. The scenery was breathtaking. It was my first time in the tropics and I'd never seen such vibrant colours: beautiful palms, bamboo, bougainvilleas, hibiscus, flame trees and frangipanis lined the roadside, with mountains rising on our right and the ocean dropping off on our left. Everyone we passed smiled and waved. Walking along in large groups in a leisurely manner, they all looked very laid back and happy.

Even the kids, who usually had to be entertained during car rides, were fascinated by the whole new world outside their windows. As we passed a school, Melina noticed the children playing in the playground wearing uniforms. 'Maman,' she asked me in French, 'will I be wearing a uniform too? What colour will it be?'

I didn't know – it hadn't come up during my endless communication back and forth with the school. My concern had been on the academic side of things: as the Fijian school year was totally different to the French one, I'd been more focused on finding out which grade Melina would fit in for the two and a half months left in this school year, and the fact that she didn't read or write English, one of the official languages of Fiji.

We were going over a bridge on the outskirts of Ba, the biggest city between Nadi and Vatukoula, when Ivan explained how when he'd been here last, the old bridge had been washed away during a particularly severe cyclone which had caused the north part of the island to be cut off for quite a while. As he was talking, I realised that I hadn't really given much thought to the dangers of cyclones, something I'd never experienced. A feeling of anxiety began creeping up on me, and my brain went into overdrive, sternly asking me what I thought I was doing, bringing my young kids to such a primitive and potentially dangerous place.

Sensing my distress, Ivan took my hand in his, smiled and said, 'It will be okay, you'll see. I know you'll come to love this place as much as I do.' I knew I could trust him, and it calmed me down. And obviously I couldn't express my anxiety in front of the children – I had to be their beacon of stability, calm and normalcy during these times of intense change, regardless of my internal doubts. I owed it to them to show strength and confidence.

In Ba, I noticed the population looked Indian. I'd been reading up about Fiji's history. The first Europeans to sight the Fiji islands were the Dutch, in 1643, and Captain James Cook, who passed the southeastern islands in 1774. William Bligh travelled through the group after the mutiny on the HMS *Bounty* in 1789 and returned to explore it in 1792.

Commercial interest in the islands began with the discovery of sandalwood at the beginning of the 19th century; tragically, within little more than a decade the accessible commercial stands of sandalwood were depleted, but by the 1820s traders were again visiting the islands to barter for sea cucumber, also known as bêche-de-mer or trepang.

By the 1860s Fiji was attracting European settlers intent on establishing plantations to capitalise on a boom in cotton prices caused by the American Civil War. In 1874, the British took control, declared Fiji a colony, and started bringing in labourers, mostly Indians, to work the sugarcane fields. By 1916 over 60 000 Indians had been relocated to Fiji. Fiji finally got its independence in 1970.

By the end of the 20th century, when we arrived in Fiji, the population consisted of two principal ethnic groups: the indigenous Melanesians, or those of mixed Melanesian-Polynesian origin; and the Indo-Fijians. Other minority groups were the Rotumans (whose home was originally the Polynesian outlier of Rotuma, situated about 500 kilometres north of the Fiji group) and the Banabans (who were moved from the island of Banaba to Rabi in eastern Fiji in 1942).

Fiji's mixed ethnicity contributed to a rich cultural heritage, with many features of traditional Fijian life evident in various ceremonies (such as the drinking of kava by Fijians and Indians alike). But the Indians of Fiji maintained their own culture, with traditional marriage ceremonies and a celebration of Diwali, the Hindu festival of lights, every October. Most Indo-Fijians were descendants of the indentured labourers, and many were very poor; most were labourers or peasant farmers. The majority were Hindu. (In 1999, about a year after our departure, Mahendra Chaudhry became Fiji's first prime minister of Indian ancestry. Fijian nationalists strongly opposed his premiership, and during his first months in office there were a number of arson and bomb attacks in Suva.)

It made for a very interesting dynamic as two very different cultures lived side by side but never mixed: an Indo-Fijian and an indigenous Fijian would never date or marry.

▲ ▲ ▲

As we kept heading north, the coastline became more rugged, with fewer and then no more beaches, just mangroves. We passed a few food stands, and Ivan pointed out a woman selling mud crabs. He told us that these crustaceans lived in the mangroves and were very tasty. We later had several opportunities to try them, and he was right – they were excellent, especially in curries.

On one occasion, while Ivan's friend Tom was in town for a few days, on a business trip from Australia, he offered to cook us a crab curry. He and Ivan went off to buy the supplies. When they got home a few hours later, the kids and I heard a commotion, and went outside to discover these two grown men screeching and pointing inside the trunk of the car: two of the bigger crabs had managed to escape and were fighting each other. One had already yanked its opponent's claw right off but the injured soldier was still on the attack. The kids and I ran back indoors, not wanting to watch any more of the carnage – or be involved in the rescue mission.

We finally passed Tavua, the last town before turning inland and travelling for another ten kilometres to reach our destination, Vatukoula, which means 'gold rock' in Fijian. This gold-mining settlement would be our home for the next two years.

Home sweet home

W e pulled up in front of a cute little yellow colonial-style bungalow surrounded by a small garden. No sooner had we stopped the car than the kids were out and running around, picking up the biggest coconuts they could find, totally amazed at the sheer thrill of finding such exotic treasures.

I headed indoors, eager to finally drop our luggage and investigate the house. It had a kitchen, a bathroom with a huge tub, which I knew the kids would enjoy, two bedrooms and a laundry area. The windows were louvre style, providing maximum air flow throughout the house, and there was an air-conditioning unit in the lounge. It had been furnished with all the basics. We really couldn't have asked for more.

We quickly unpacked our suitcases, and the kids lined up all their teddies on their beds.

A knock at the front door turned out to be Mick and Judy, the couple next door, who'd come over to welcome us. Looking to be about in their mid-fifties, and Australian, Judy had a huge smile and was holding a plate of cookies (she quickly became Melina and Mansell's best friend!), while Mick spoke a mile a minute in a very strong accent. They were both extremely friendly, offering to help with anything we needed, and we instantly loved them and knew we'd be good friends. Indeed, Judy and I became inseparable.

My first night in our new surroundings felt very strange, with lots of noises I didn't recognise. One in particular made me jump and sit up straight, heart pounding. It sounded like someone was screaming outside our window. I quickly shook Ivan awake, telling him to go see who was there. He was back a few minutes later, not having seen anything suspicious, and settled back into bed.

When the unearthly scream came again, he burst out laughing. Leading me gently to the window, he pointed at a little gecko sitting outside. 'There's the culprit,' he said. I couldn't believe that such a small animal could make such a loud noise.

The next morning, on very little sleep, I made my way to the kitchen for a cup of coffee. There, standing nonchalantly on the counter, was the biggest cockroach I'd ever seen. I've got a phobia about creepy-crawlies, and I let out a huge scream. Everyone came running. When my kids realised what the problem was, Melina said, 'Don't worry, Mummy, you go back to bed, we'll make him disappear.'

I didn't hesitate, running back to bed and burying my head under the pillows. A big commotion ensued, mixed with some laughter, until eventually all seemed quiet again and they yelled to me, 'You can come out now, Mum!'

In the kitchen, Ivan and the kids looked very pleased with themselves. Ivan handed me a freshly brewed cup of coffee. 'Welcome to the tropics,' he said.

But soon my attention was occupied with a much more curious matter, when Ivan went to answer a knock on the front door and came back with a strange look on his face.

'Who was that?' I asked him.

'Mick,' he answered, quickly crossing the kitchen and pulling the curtains closed.

'Why didn't you ask him in for a cup of coffee ... and why are you closing the curtains?' I asked, wondering what was going on.

At that moment a short, high-pitched squeal shattered the early-morning peace.

'Oh my god!' I whispered, aware of not terrifying the children. 'What was that?'

'Well,' Ivan said, 'it's a Fijian tradition for parties and celebrations to have a pig roast, and it turns out that today is our other neighbour, Semi's, eldest son's birthday. Mick was heading out to his car when he saw the poor animal being dragged down the street, and he came to warn us that the slaughter was about to take place on our neighbours' front lawn.'

'Oh boy,' I muttered, pouring myself a second cup of coffee. 'And it's only 10 am on our first day.'

▲ ▲ ▲

I never completely got over my insect phobia but after a few weeks, as I became more familiar with my new surroundings, my family's morning ritual of sweeping the house for unwelcome visitors could stop, and I came to realise that creepy-crawlies were part of life in the tropics.

Our much-loved neighbours. Mick was a brilliant handyman and spent all his spare time in his garage, tinkering with machines and building things. Judy had a great deal of experience living abroad as a mining wife and a mother, and I looked up to her.

Going shopping

I was feeling quite excited about our plans to go into the town of Tavua, ten kilometres back down the Kings Road, to explore the grocery stores and markets. We had quite an extensive shopping list, and I couldn't help but wonder how many of the items we'd be able to find in a small town on an island in the middle of the Pacific. Nutella, for example – it was a staple breakfast item in our house, and also part of the first-aid kit and often the solution to little upsets, used to settle small arguments and occasionally as a negotiation tool. I'd brought some with me and thank goodness the Fijian customs had been kind enough not to confiscate it, but we'd definitely need to restock. And what about cheese? I wouldn't be picky and expect a double-cream brie or roquefort, but some cheddar would be nice.

By noon we were out the door, heading back down the dirt road for about three kilometres before turning right onto the paved road leading into the town. The road was in poor condition, and Ivan had to concentrate to dodge the bigger potholes.

It was a very dusty town, and even the vegetation didn't look as vibrant here, covered as it was in thick yellow dust. The shops lined one side of the main street, including a video store and a bank (with a long line of workers outside, patiently waiting their turn), with an intricate temple and a few homes along the other. People were mingling on the pavement, which was in no better state than the road.

We parked the car and headed up the street to familiarise ourselves with what would become our main shopping area. We walked past a store selling mostly fabric, but also very frilly dresses, which Melina was immediately attracted to, pulling me in for a look. The man behind the counter welcomed us, indicating to his sales associate to attend to us.

She was so hot on our heels that as I turned to look at something that had caught my eye, I bumped right into her. Ignoring my apologies, she turned her focus on Melina, trying to entice her with all kinds of glittery, girly things. 'We're just browsing, we're not going to buy anything,' I told her, but she was unfazed, continuing to press items onto my young daughter. Nothing turns me off more than the feeling of being pressured, so we made our way back to the door, waved goodbye and escaped.

Rejoining Ivan and Mansell outside, I told Ivan what had happened, and he grimaced. 'I'm afraid you're going to have to get used to that,' he said, then added, laughing, 'I'm not sure which is worse, this or the French nonexistent customer service.'

We strolled on, debating the pros and cons of aggressive versus indifferent sales assistants, until I was stopped dead in my tracks by something in a shop window. Jaw dropping, I pointed to the central display in what turned out to be the window of the hardware store. Huge signs pointed to the not-to-be-missed bargain of the week which was not, as might have been expected, cans of paint or drills, but a large wooden coffin.

'What's that, Mum?' asked our 4-year-old.

'A chest to store toys in,' Ivan said quickly, taking Mansell's hand and moving on towards the butcher shop.

We ventured in purely out of curiosity – we'd been advised to buy our meat from a butcher in Nadi, which supplied all the hotels and restaurants with a good selection of beef, pork, sausages and chicken. And I offered up a little prayer of thanks for this as I read the very first sign the customer would see on entering the shop: 'Please do not spit in this store.'

'Yuk,' I said.

Ivan laughed. 'Well, I'm glad to see sanitation measures are being enforced.'

The next sign read, 'White people is better than corned beef.'

I turned to Ivan for an explanation, and he informed me that Fiji was once known as the Cannibal Isles! I could feel the blood draining from my face as I asked him in a shaky voice, 'Do they still eat humans?'

'No, no, don't worry,' he responded, reassuringly, 'these practices stopped long, long ago, back in the 1800s. People still like to make jokes about it, though.'

I believed him, but I still kept a tight hold of my two little kids, just in case.

We finally got to the supermarket, which was nothing like I was used to, and at first glance I didn't recognise any products. The face creams advertised 'whitening' rather than wrinkle repair; the fruit and veggie section seemed to be from another world altogether, selling taro, breadfruit and cassava; and even my basic

Cannibalism has a long history in the Fijian Islands. The last known act of cannibalism occurred in 1867, when Methodist missionary Reverend Thomas Baker, along with six Fijian student teachers, was murdered and eaten.

herbs, like thyme, oregano and rosemary, had been supplanted by ginger, cumin and curry powder.

Struggling to keep my composure and not show that I felt totally overwhelmed, I walked up and down the aisles in a trance, glancing down at my grocery list and sighing, as now realised I wouldn't find half of what was on there.

The dairy aisle was very small and disappointing, with all the yoghurts past their use-by date; I chose the newest ones and hoped for the best. And I did find some cheddar – for which I was ever so grateful, as I know this small victory prevented another internal breakdown.

Ivan and the kids had taken their own trolley, and when I bumped into them at the Coca-Cola fridge (something I recognised!), they seemed to have been much more successful than I – until I looked closer and realised that most of their items were cookies, chocolates, cereal and juice!

▲ ▲ ▲

I had much higher hopes for the local food market. I loved markets of all kinds but especially the fresh food ones, which had been part of French culture for centuries.

In Carcassonne, the farmers, producers and vendors invaded the town square three times a week, with the biggest market on Saturdays. Restaurants and coffee shops relinquished their prime real estate on the square till noon, at which point the municipal cleaning crew descended in force to give it a thorough sweep and wash before the tables and chairs were reinstalled and life could resume. It was a fascinating logistical operation to witness and – surprisingly in a country in which the favourite pastime is to complain – nobody ever moaned about the upheaval.

Market day was also gossip day – a time to not only pick up groceries but also to meet up and discuss the latest news, usually in a very agitated, loud and expressive manner, whether it be about politics (everyone had an opinion), sport (how terribly the team had done), the latest news stories or just the weather.

After the world had been put to rights, the shoppers would move on to picking their products. This took focus and a keen eye for the perfect tomato, peach or apple. All items had to be thoroughly examined, touched and smelt before any money changed hands. The vendors were always passionate about their goods, explaining in detail how they produced the cheese, salami, olives, honey, oil or bread they were selling, and usually allowing tasting. Their enthusiasm was infectious and rarely did anyone leave a stall without something of whatever was being sold.

But the food market in Tavua was, once again, not at all what I was expecting: dotted around a floor of compacted soil were a cluster of rickety tables covered by torn tarps that had probably been through several cyclones; stray dogs sniffed for scraps under the tables. The smells were mostly Indian spices, with a strong overlay of cloves, and tobacco. The noise was deafening, with hundreds of chickens clucking, dogs barking, cars honking and people shouting.

I'd lost sight of Ivan and just stood there, holding on to the two little ones, taking in my surroundings, feeling as if all my senses were being attacked. The kids were pinching their noses against the unfamiliar smells.

Ivan finally appeared, grinning, but his smile soon faded as he took a look at us three and realised how overwhelmed we were. 'I'm so sorry,' he said. 'I forgot that all this is totally new to you. Come, let me introduce you and the kids around to people I know here from before. I've found some delicious treats that I'm sure you're going to love.'

Reluctantly at first, we followed him, and, sure enough, with some time and explanations, we started appreciating the people and the interactions. Fijians love kids, and they were all attracted to our two little people, stroking Melina's long straight hair and doing high-fives with Mansell, and treating them to pieces of fresh coconut and pineapple. The children loved it, and I also started enjoying myself, discovering fruit and vegetables I didn't recognise. Ivan was telling jokes that made the women burst out laughing, holding their bellies. It was such a beautiful sight.

At a colourful Indian sweet stand, we examined items that looked like fried dough covered in an incredibly red syrup. Called gulab jamun, they turned out to be delicious, and the kids made me promise to buy them every time we came here. Another favourite were the mangoes, which were plump, juicy and amazingly tasty.

I spotted some beautiful cherries, and as I was filling a paper bag, Ivan came over. 'Are you sure you want so many of those?' he asked. 'They're the hottest chillies here.'

I quickly apologised to the vendor, and left with a more sensible quantity of the bright-red peppers.

Heading back to the car, laden down with fresh fruits,

vegetables and treats, I realised that in fact this market wasn't that different from the ones I knew in France: here, like there, people were connecting around their love of food.

Off to school

'**I** graduated with a teaching diploma a few years back and was lucky enough to land a good position in a nice school on the Gold Coast of Australia, but after a couple years I started getting restless. I didn't feel I was challenging myself enough, so when I spotted the ad for this position in the newspaper, I applied. Of course, I first had to convince my wife, who wasn't as taken with the idea as me, and was concerned about the wellbeing of our 2-year-old daughter.'

Paul Grey, the young principal of Goldfields Primary School, was explaining how he'd ended up as the head of this tiny school of just 35 pupils ranging from grade one to grade seven. Tall and softly spoken, Paul hadn't been in the position long.

Fiji had a high literacy rate, with most children between the ages of 6 and 13 attending the free primary schools. The language of instruction was English and corporal punishment was still allowed.

Goldfields Primary School, which accommodated only the children of the mine's employees, was small but nonetheless offered an international-standard education following the Australian curriculum. And it was conveniently located only a short walk from what would be our permanent home.

'I totally get it!' I said. 'And may I ask how you're finding it?'

'Oh, we love it! It's such a beautiful place, and a very easygoing lifestyle, and a great environment to bring up a family.'

It was only ten days since our arrival, so I was really thrilled to hear Paul's positive feedback about living here with children.

He was giving us a guided tour over a weekend, in preparation for school starting on the Monday. Turning to Melina, he said, 'I'm sure you're curious to see your new classroom?'

Melina nodded but didn't say a word. Since Ivan had entered our lives, her English had improved tremendously, and she was comfortable having conversations, but she wasn't as keen on the reading and writing. I was confident that once school started, she'd quickly catch up with her peers.

'We have two teachers, a husband and wife, Mr and Mrs Peters,' Paul continued, still speaking to Melina. 'They're both Fijians but were educated in Australia. Mrs Peters takes grades one to four – she'll be your teacher – and Mr Peters and I share grades five, six and seven.'

Turning to Ivan and me, Paul said, 'As we have so few students, having different grades within one classroom isn't an issue. Everyone gets some one-on-one time with the teacher. Also, we encourage parents to volunteer their time in the classroom, especially with reading, if that's something you'd like to do?'

'Absolutely! I'd love that, thank you!' I answered cheerfully, as I'd been thinking about how I was going to fill my days.

The three classrooms were each furnished with individual desks and chairs facing a blackboard, with the teacher's desk by the window. Melina's classroom had several educational posters on the walls, as well as kids' colourful paintings, and this could have been any young children's classroom anywhere in the world – except that there was no glass in the windows, and the ceiling fans turned constantly, making the heat a little bit more bearable.

Melina was putting on a brave face, but I could tell she was nervous by the way she shuffled from one foot to the other while biting her lower lip. My heart went out to her and I felt my eyes sting with held-back tears.

At that moment, a little girl with curly blonde hair came running up the path. 'I'm here!' she called.

'Melina, this is Nina, who'll be in your class. She'll show you around outside, if you like?'

'I'd love that!' Melina said, and as I watched the two of them walking into the playground, chatting away, I felt a huge weight lifting off my shoulders.

'She'll do just fine,' said Paul, looking at me with a smile. 'She's a bright little girl, and she'll adapt very quickly.'

A ten-minute drive from the school was the little house, not much different from ours, where Mansell would be spending every weekday morning at Vatukoula Preschool. It had a wooden fence with a small gate, and we called out to the woman standing in the garden. As she came over to welcome us in, I could see that she was from Rotuma. She had beautiful Polynesian features, with long straight hair and paler skin that that of the indigenous Fijians, and her whole demeanour was calm, gentle and loving.

Spying Mansell, she immediately bent down and opened her

arms. 'Hello young man, how are you? My name is Miss Levatu. What is your name?'

▲ ▲ ▲

Monday morning, the first day of school in a foreign country and, for my kids, a foreign language, finally arrived. I'd been dreading this day, when my two little ones would be thrown in the deep end, and required to swim, no sinking allowed.

'I don't want to go to school. I want to stay home with you, Mummy,' Mansell said, holding his toy lion, Simba, in a death grip.

'I know, my sweetie,' I said, keeping my voice very enthusiastic and upbeat to hide my own fears, 'but just think of all the new friends you're going to meet and play with! Also, I'm sure they have a lot more toys at school than we have at home – it will be so much fun!'

That was certainly true – most of the kids' toys were still on their way over in the shipping container, but Mansell wasn't to be persuaded. 'Anyway, Mummy, I can't find my shoes-on,' he said, pouting.

Like his sister's, his English was coming along nicely, and I loved it when they sometimes got the wording wrong – it was so cute. Mansell had decided that shoes were actually called 'shoes-on', because Mummy was always saying, 'Put your shoes on.'

I bent down, gave him a big hug and said, 'Come on, sweetie, let me help you look for them. Then I'll make you a Nutella sandwich.'

During the week before term resumed, and while Ivan was at work, the kids and I had got acquainted with our neighbourhood.

We'd go on walks, watch the local kids play ball, pick flowers (all heavenly scented; gardenias were Melina's favourite) and collect giant leaves with Mansell, who would use them to build a tent in our back yard. All three of us were in awe of the vegetation around us.

We quickly learnt to keep our eyes open on our walks when a coconut came crashing down only inches from my head. The kids couldn't wait to tell Ivan how scary it had been, and he explained that yes, they were a hazard, and joked that maybe we should be wearing hardhats on our nature walks!

On the first day of school, Ivan took the morning off work to accompany me on the first drop-off. I needed all the support I could get; I had a huge lump in my throat and my stomach was in a knot.

At the primary school, Melina spotted Nina walking in with her brother and asked for permission to join them. As we watched her run ahead, Ivan took my hand and we looked at each other, letting out a big sigh of relief. We caught up to them at the classroom, where Mrs Peters was introducing Melina to the other students. 'Melina comes all the way from France,' she was saying. 'Let's all say hello and make her feel welcome.'

'Bula vinaka, Melina!' they all yelled, and although my little girl turned bright red, I spotted a twinkle in her eye, a good sign that she was loving the attention.

On the short drive to the preschool, Mansell was still trying to negotiate a few extra days with me. 'I really don't see why I can't stay with you. You're going to be so lonely all by yourself,' he reasoned. Refusing to give in, I pointed out the window at the beautiful landscape we were driving through: a woman was hanging out washing on lines tied between two huge palms while little kids ran between the sheets playing hide-and-seek, chickens pecked at food and dogs rummaged through some overturned rubbish bins.

We arrived at the little house, and Miss Levatu came out to meet us. Mansell retreated behind me, holding tightly to my leg.

After greeting us both, Miss Levatu winked at me. 'Tell me, Mansell,' she said, crouching down so she could catch his eye. 'Do you by any chance like chocolate? Because it's Tomasi's birthday today and his mum has brought a big chocolate cake for us to share and celebrate with him. Would you like a piece?'

It was a masterstroke. 'Yes, please! Chocolate is my favourite food in the whole world,' Mansell told her.

'Well, hurry up, we must get inside before it's all gone.'

He slowly walked forward and took her hand, and together they walked into the little house. I followed, my heart melting.

The little preschool classroom was neat and tidy, with several play stations set up, a painting table, an area dedicated to crafts, and a big blackboard on the wall. There was a well-stocked bookshelf with a large colourful rug in front of it. As in Melina's classroom, there were no windowpanes, and two big ceiling fans moved the humid air around. The playground was gorgeous, set in lush tropical greens, and with a slide, a toboggan, a swing set and a sandpit.

The children, about twenty of them, were all gathered around the star of the day, little Tomasi, and I was delighted to see Mansell standing among them, lustily singing 'Happy Birthday', his eyes focused entirely on the cake. Ivan and I waved and blew him a goodbye kiss, and he hardly noticed us leaving.

▲ ▲ ▲

That evening around the kitchen table the atmosphere was much lighter than it had been at breakfast. The children were talking over each other, full of stories about their experiences, their new friends and their teachers.

We couldn't have wished for a better first day.

Meeting Melita

T he second school morning went off smoothly too, with only a few tears from Mansell and no more than ten questions from Melina. She was a little worrywart and needed confirmation that, yes, I would be on time for pickup at exactly 3 pm.

Back at home, around mid-morning, I finished my cup of coffee and decided I'd tackle the laundry. My own modern front-loader was still on the high seas along with the rest of our belongings, a month away from making landfall on Fiji, but I'd noticed a washing machine in the laundry room. Now, looking at it more closely, I realised I'd never seen anything quite like it. I didn't think that even my grandmother would've had something so primitive.

It had two tubs, a hosepipe and a timer. Basically, you filled the first tub with water, put your clothes in along with the detergent, then set the timer for twenty minutes. The tub started shaking and vibrating, making the most horrendous noise and sounding like the whole thing might blow up. When the timer went off, you had to drain the water out of the first tub, fill the second tub with clean water for rinsing, transfer the sopping clothes into the second tub, and reset the timer, this time for ten minutes.

'There's no bloody way I'm doing this for a whole month,' I

muttered to myself, exhausted and irritated, wiping sweat and foam off my forehead. I went outside and sat, fed up, on the front step.

A car pulled up outside the house and the driver hooted cheerfully. It was Allan, Ivan's boss. 'Hi Fiona!' he called out the window. 'I've brought you some help.'

A beautiful, tall young woman got out of the passenger side. 'Bula vinaka!' she yelled.

'This is Melita, and she's going to be your housemaid,' Allan called. 'I have to get going, so I'll leave you two to it!' And with that, he disappeared in a cloud of dust.

Ivan had told me we would have a house cleaner. I'd tried to argue that we wouldn't need one, as I wasn't going to be working, and was quite happy to deal with household chores – it would occupy my days and save us the money. But Ivan explained that it was kind of an unwritten rule: when you came to work in their country, you provided work for at least one local person, if not more, depending on the size of your property.

'You couldn't have arrived at a better time!' I said to Melita, and guided her to the laundry room, where the big old twin tub was shaking and wheezing and emitting puffs of foam.

She let out a huge belly laugh and shook her head. 'This machine is infamous!' she said. 'It's been part of the welcome package for most newcomers.'

'Well, it's definitely unique,' I conceded.

'Don't worry, I'll sort it out,' Melita said, confidently. 'I have quite a lot of experience using it.'

I made us both a cup of coffee, and we sat down to get to know each other. Melita told me she had three young children and was the only breadwinner for her family, as her husband was on strike and had been for the past two years! He and a few other men had been upset by the mine's previous management team, and had walked off the job, but despite changes at the top and new regulations, several, including him, had decided to keep striking.

'To be honest, I think he's just too lazy to go back to work,' Melita said, between sips of coffee. 'He spends his time fishing, so most days he brings home fish for dinner. As long as my children are happy and healthy, I'm happy.'

As we were sitting there, we noticed a young boy walking through the garden. Melita got up and went outside to talk to him, and by the sound of it, she wasn't happy with him.

Coming back into the kitchen, she said, 'Sorry about that. The young people don't respect private property. You should consider getting a dog. Fijians are scared of dogs, and it would deter them from trespassing.'

I liked the idea of getting a dog, and not just to deter trespassers. 'The kids would love that!' I said. 'I'll speak to Ivan about it when he comes in for lunch. Maybe he knows where we can get one.'

'Mr Allan was telling me on our drive here that his dog has just recently had puppies. Maybe he can bring one over to you,' Melita suggested.

'Thanks for letting me know. Ivan can talk to him about it.'

When Ivan had lived here before, he'd had a dog called Duke. Ivan told me how twice a year the community would round up stray dogs, and residents were also invited to bring their pets to the bowling club, where mass sterilisations would be performed by a couple of vets from Suva, the capital, with the pool table serving as the operating table. Ivan said he would never forget the look his poor old Duke gave him as he was coming out of the anesthesia after he'd been castrated; it was as if to say, 'And you call yourself my friend?!'

Once our drinks were done, we both got on with some chores, Melita tackling the laundry while I sorted the kids' rooms. I could hear her singing a Fijian song while working, a melodious and pretty tune.

I was happy to have Melita in the house, and it became our ritual to start each day sitting at the kitchen table with a cup of coffee each, talking about our lives but mostly about our children.

▲ ▲ ▲

During our morning chats, Melita would often talk about Fijian customs and traditions. One of these was the KereKere system, which all villages relied on. The concept was very simple: for a village to thrive, it needs its people to pull together, and if one is down on his luck or in need of something, the others chip in.

'So, you see, if you have an item that a neighbour or relative needs, he or she can ask you for it, and if you agree, no payment is expected in return. Then, one day, when that neighbour or relative has something you need, the favour can be returned.'

'That's so nice!' I said.

'Yes, in principle, it is perfect. But it does have its flaws. More often than not, the person will just take the item without permission, and it always seems to be the same people doing the taking, and the same being taken advantage of.'

And, indeed, during our time in Fiji, I had two experiences with the KereKere. The first was about a month after our arrival, when my favourite T-shirt went missing. It wouldn't have seemed special to anyone else – it was just a touristy T-shirt with a drawing of a smiley face wearing a bandana and 'Wild about Carcassonne' inscribed across the front. I'd picked it up at the markets before leaving Carcassonne, and I loved wearing it because it felt like a link to my old life, a kind of life jacket. I know it sounds ridiculous, but having it sitting in my closet kept me balanced, a bit like my kids with their favourite teddy bears.

I turned my whole wardrobe upside down and there was no sign of the garment. As soon as Melita arrived for work that morning, I told her about it, and described the T-shirt in detail. I felt silly about how upset I was about it, but she appeared to make no judgement, and promised she would keep an eye out for it.

A few days after our conversation, one morning I noticed the T-shirt back on top of the pile in my cupboard. I never did ask Melita how she'd got it back, but I guessed she must have bumped into the person wearing it, and explained how this item was excluded from KereKere.

A few months later, almost all my bras disappeared. I never really paid attention to the number I had in the drawer; I would just grab and go. I'm not very French when it comes to that – I've never been a fine-lingerie kind of person, and as long as it does its job and it's comfortable, with no underwire poking into me, I'm happy. But on this particular day, as I reached into the drawer, there was only one bra there. I asked Melita if she'd seen any bras in the wash, but, alas, no.

It seemed that someone had helped themselves off our clothes line. To me, this wasn't KereKere but theft, pure and simple. It was a valuable lesson: from then on, I made sure my smalls were hung up to dry in the bathroom, never too far out of sight.

I tried to find replacement bras in Tavua but none quite fit properly, and the situation became desperate. Luckily for me, Judy was due to nip over to her homeland for a quick visit with her daughters, and kindly offered to go shopping on my behalf. I was eternally grateful.

Although Ivan never had any items 'KereKereed', he told me about the time he brought a rugby shirt back from Australia, for a young Fijian boy who caddied for him when he played golf. The poor boy never got to wear the shirt, and it got passed around the whole village, a different person wearing it each day. Ivan nicknamed it 'the communal shirt'.

Finding out about Fiji

Judy, myself and three other women attended classes to learn some basic Fijian. These took place at the local high school. Although English was one of the official languages, the other two were Fijian and Fiji Hindi (which is very different from Indian Hindi). We felt it right to try and communicate in the local language.

The early missionaries had picked the Bau dialect as the standard language for printing and communicating, partly because it was the language of the politically dominant island of Bau. By the 19th century, it had been adopted by the British administration and over time it evolved into the standard Fijian of today, which includes many English and other dialectal words. For example, an English catchphrase that summarised life in Fiji and always made me smile was 'No hurry, no worry' – in other words, you're now on 'island time'.

As a celebration for the five of us completing our six-lesson course, our teacher invited us to partake in a kava ceremony. This ceremony was used as a celebration, including in formal settings, such as when the prime minister welcomed dignitaries from other countries, and also served for conflict resolution, settling arguments between people or villages.

Ivan had a good laugh at me when I got home – I didn't have to tell him what we'd done, as he guessed by looking at my dopey, silly smile. I could also always tell when he'd been to a work kava ceremony, which was at least twice a month.

I told Melita the next time she came that I'd attended a kava ceremony.

She laughed. 'I bet you felt good afterwards.'

'Yes,' I said, 'very relaxed. Maybe too relaxed!'

'Well, it's meant to relax you, make you feel happy,' she said. 'It can also be used for its medicinal properties; it reduces pain and can stop seizures.'

'I was very worried about drinking that untreated water, but I didn't experience any side effects,' I admitted.

We had a rainwater tank attached to our house that provided us with water that came out of a separate tap at the kitchen sink. I'd been shown how to filter the water by putting a piece of cloth over the end of the tap to collect all the mosquito larvae and other undesirables, and I would change it once a week and never took a look at what might be in it, to stop myself from totally freaking out. I'd then boil the water for ten minutes before pouring it into bottles, and this was the safe drinking water for the family.

'But when I saw we were all going to drink out of the same cup, I just told myself not to worry,' I said.

Melita chuckled and said, 'You can consider yourself lucky that nowadays the roots are crushed by hand. In the olden days, they were crushed by chewing!' Then she turned serious and said, 'We women don't like to take part in the kava drinking. It's more something men do. Plus, over time, it can cause liver damage.'

'I'm glad I got to try it and the ritual that surrounds it, but I'm not that keen on doing it again,' I told her.

One thing Ivan and I agreed on is how hard it was to sit cross-legged for an extended time. My ceremony took only fifty minutes but some last hours. Luckily, kava numbs the aches and pains.

▲ ▲ ▲

I had a few errands to run in town, so the kids and I hopped into the car and headed to Tavua.

Our first stop, as usual, was the markets, to get fresh pine-apple and some Indian sweets for the little ones. Then I had to draw cash, so we headed over to the bank. They didn't have a bank machine, so I went up to the teller.

'Bula,' I said.

She said nothing but nodded and smiled.

'I'd like to get some cash out of my account, please.'

She typed something into the computer, then looked at the key-pad on my side of the counter and lifted her eyebrows. I inserted the card, then, following the prompts, typed in my amount and PIN.

She put the money into the little drawer between us, and pushed it towards me, flicking her eyebrows twice to indicate that I could take the money. Then she pushed a receipt through and with a little head movement and a slightly longer lift of one eye-brow, indicated that I should sign it.

Transaction completed, I said, 'Thank you,' and she nodded

and smiled. Then, looking past me to the next person standing in the queue, she lifted her eyebrows again, indicating that they could approach.

As we left the bank, Melina asked, 'Mummy, do you think that lady had a sore throat? She never said a word!'

'No, sweetie,' I said. 'I think she was just very efficient.'

I told Ivan about this experience, and he laughed and said that he had the exact same interaction with his crew at work. 'It's weird, no words are exchanged and yet the message comes across loud and clear,' he said, describing precisely what I'd felt during the exchange with the bank teller.

It became a game Ivan and I played – trying to only use our eyebrows to communicate. He won every time: he has extremely expressive brows!

▲ ▲ ▲

The kids and I were at home one afternoon when we got a rather unusual visit. Ambling past my kitchen window was a big bull, or bulumakau in Fijian. He'd wandered into the back yard and was munching on tufts of grass.

Cows in Fiji are a sign of wealth. Melita told me that she owned seven of them. When the owners didn't have land on which to keep their cows, they just tied them up by the side of the road. I could see the long cord the bull was dragging behind him, so I assumed he'd gotten loose from somewhere.

Unfortunately, Melita wasn't at the house on this particular day to help. The kids and I walked out onto our back deck, keeping an eye on the huge animal and hoping he would soon find his own way out. It wouldn't be that simple, however, as our dog, Shadow, suddenly woke up and became determined to defend her property against the intruder.

An angry barking and mooing match ensued, with no real winner. The bulumakau, who was getting really irate, suddenly ran down the garden, and unfortunately his cord wrapped around the garden tap as he went.

I rang Ivan and was busy explaining the situation to him when the bull yanked himself free, taking the tap with him. A huge water jet exploded out of the ground, making Shadow scurry away in fright and the bull even more upset.

'I'm calling the security team to head over straight away,' Ivan told me.

'You'd better send a plumber too!' I shouted.

The kids and I were kept very entertained watching five security guards spend some hours trying to catch the angry bulumakau, all the while slipping and sliding down the muddy hill. It made for a great story for Melina to share with her class the next day.

▲ ▲ ▲

Rugby is the national sport of not only Fiji but many other southern Pacific islands, like Samoa, Tonga and the most famous one, New Zealand. Everywhere you look in Fiji, in every city and town, in even the most remote village in the interior, you'll see children playing rugby. Most play barefoot, using a plastic bottle instead of a ball.

It wasn't unusual for cows and bulls to get loose and wander through the town – yet another hazard for unwary drivers.

Ivan and I would always comment on how it seemed that the minute school was done for the day, the kids were out chasing that ball until the sun went down and they could no longer see. We marvelled at the simplicity of their life, and at how happy these kids were compared to those in our society, with their gadgets and material things. Kids from first-world countries seemed not to know how to entertain themselves any more. They were all glued to the TV or playing video games, and still moped around complaining about having nothing to do.

I wasn't naive enough to think that the Fijian children would still prefer to play outside if they too had access to TV and video games, but I actually found myself feeling sorry for the 'rich kids' who were becoming ever more antisocial, lazy and stressed from the lack of outdoor exercise. I wanted to pull my hair out when even my own children told me that video games were considered a sport.

So it's no surprise that Fiji has such a strong national rugby union team. The problem was that they struggled to retain players to play for the national team, as many had contracts in Europe, where the pay was good. Unfortunately, money rules the world and it was just much more lucrative to play overseas.

The HSBC World Rugby Sevens series is a lot of fun on and off the pitch. It's held in ten locations, from Europe and the Middle East, to Asia, North America, South Africa and Australia, with sixteen national teams competing over two days. Fiji always does very well in this tournament, with the Fiji Sevens' unorthodox style of play earning the team the nickname the 'Flying Fijians'. The Flying Fijians have competed in the World Rugby Sevens

Series, the Rugby World Cup Sevens and the Olympics, and they won the gold medal at the 2016 Summer Olympics in Brazil.

While we were in Fiji, we were lucky to get the chance to go to one of the events. The atmosphere was electric on the pitch, due to the fast pace and short games (lasting only fourteen minutes each), and in the stands, where supporters were encouraged to come dressed up in costumes, making the ambiance even more exhilarating.

Of course, Fiji supporters led the way in the entertainment and music spectacle, singing, dancing and banging their drums for two days straight.

Watching the local kids exercising, developing a team spirit, forming friendships and having fun always brought me immense joy.

Settling in

Although we lived in a remote place, we still found ways to entertain ourselves. One woman was an excellent cross-stitcher and offered classes, while others volunteered to teach us to play chess or bridge, and many held cooking lessons. But the main entertainment in Vatukoula was golf.

The nine-hole golf course, located inside a dormant volcano, was considered challenging. There were two seasons in Fiji, wet and dry, and the course would change dramatically depending on the time of year you were playing.

Hole number 6 was probably the most challenging of all, and even the best of players dreaded it: you had to tee off from the bottom of an incredibly steep hill and land on the green at the top. In the dry season, if you didn't hit the ball hard enough to clear the top, you would have to watch its increasingly speedy descent as it came rolling down and often way past where you were standing. In the wet, however, the ball would land and sit even on the steepest of places; and at times it would simply disappear into the quagmire, never to be seen again.

Most of our socialising was done at the clubhouse, located on a hilltop. It consisted of a wooden structure with a bar, a big, open indoor space and a huge outdoor deck overlooking the course. No matter the season, there was always a gentle breeze blowing, making the humidity more bearable.

The mine was a 24/7 operation but on weekends management would take turns being on call, allowing the rest of the team some time off. They would tee off in groups of four, making it back to the clubhouse a couple of hours later, when their families would join them for drinks.

Young Fijians would come up from the nearby villages to offer their services as caddies, getting an opportunity of making a few extra dollars, and also sometimes to play a round of golf. Fijians are, on the whole, naturally gifted at sport and would often enjoy challenging the expats to a game.

Ivan told me about the time his caddy arrived wearing only one shoe. 'What happened to your other shoe?' he asked.

'Oh, nothing,' came the cheerful reply. 'I found this shoe on the way here.'

Ivan said, 'It really made me realise how much we take for granted. My first thought was that he'd lost a shoe because, for me, everyone has shoes. I never thought of someone not having a pair of shoes and being so happy finding just one.'

Weekends would start early, as the offices closed by 4 pm on Fridays to give staff and their spouses and partners a chance to fit in a game of golf before night fell. Fiji is located fairly close to the equator, so regardless of the time of year, it was always dark by 7 pm. I had trouble adjusting to that at first, as, for me, warmer weather usually meant longer days.

Friday nights were the highlight of the week, and always a

jovial time. Work would be left behind and a good time would be had by all. The kids would all run around together, chasing cane toads (with strict instructions, of course, to not touch them, as they secrete potentially lethal venom from their glands), and playing hide-and-seek or whatever new game the elder ones came up with. The adults would share a few beers or glasses of wine, swapping stories about their adventures in the tropics.

Raj, a soft-spoken Indo-Fijian, was the barman and clubhouse manager. He was extremely efficient, and kept the drinks flowing. And on Friday evenings, he would sell delicious vegetable-curry rotis prepared by his wife. My kids quickly acquired a taste for curry and spices, and within six months were eating the rotis along with us.

The evening would go on in a relaxed, casual atmosphere, while we chatted, listened to music, danced and played cards.

I met the rest of the Vatukoula wives at these Friday get-togethers. Many of them were older, with children who were either grown up or at school in Australia or New Zealand. I couldn't imagine sending my children so far away and only seeing them three times a year. I told Ivan in no uncertain terms that this wasn't going to happen in our family. We were a long way from having to make that kind of decision, but I wanted him to know my point of view. I'd attended boarding school for a year and absolutely hated it. And as a mum, maybe selfishly, I wanted to keep my kids close for as long I could. They grow up so fast.

One of these women, Bernadette, was a Kaivalagi, a 'white Fijian'. Born and brought up in Fiji, she obviously spoke fluent

Fijian, and I loved spending time with her and learning about her childhood.

She, Judy, myself and a few others started going out for a game of golf after school drop-offs. I'd never played golf and it became very quickly apparent that I wasn't a natural. In fact, I wasn't good at any sports involving hitting balls, something I'd discovered the hard way when I was about 10 years old and my parents signed me up for tennis lessons. A group of us faced the ball-launching machine after the instructor had demonstrated the technique – all we had to do was copy him. I missed the ball every single time. When asked by my parents about my progress and I explained the situation, they took me to an ophthalmologist who concluded that I had a lazy eye which, combined with my strabismus (a condition in which the eyes don't properly align with each other), meant I battled with depth perception and would therefore always have difficulty with hand-eye coordination. Well, that was my excuse and I stuck to it!

It didn't stop me from trying different sports throughout my life, though, and here I was, giving it my all at golf. Despite many air swings and a horrendous score sheet, I enjoyed the exercise and the beautiful walk. I felt as if I was inside a *National Geographic*. The gorgeous vegetation was home to some spectacular birds, with parrots (which I'd only ever seen in pet stores before) flying free all around us.

But it was another kind of animal that gave me a nasty experience on the golf course. One morning, as I was setting myself up to tee off, focusing on the job at hand, eyeing the direction I wanted the ball to follow, and making sure my arms were straight,

58

my knees bent and my feet parallel, I suddenly felt the most excruciating burning sensation in my legs and arms. Looking down, I was horrified to see what seemed to be millions of little red ants crawling all over my legs, hands and arms – it turned out I was standing right on top of an ants' nest.

As I screamed and slapped at myself, my friends jumped into the fight to get them off me, hitting and swiping at me. We must have looked like we were performing some kind of ritual dance and song, but I can tell you, I've never been in so much burning pain in my life!

The second time I made a spectacle of myself during a game of golf was entirely my own doing. For once, I wasn't doing too badly, but then my ball landed by a tree with a big patch of weeds in front of it. Having calculated the best way forward, I swung my club high above me – hitting the branch above so hard that I broke my club in two. I never lived that one down.

Some very entertaining golf tournaments were organised two or three times a year. In one, called Best Ball, we would play in groups of four, mixing weaker players with stronger ones. Every player started from the same spot and we would all continue from the spot where the best-placed ball landed. All the players had to wear sulus, or sarongs, which meant that men and women alike played in very colourful skirts. I'd never seen my husband in a skirt before, and I discovered he had great legs despite the fact that they were very, very hairy.

▲ ▲ ▲

The golf course landscape was spectacular –
very hilly, with breathtaking views.

In France, schools provided a hot meal served at the canteen, for which parents paid a minimal fee. It wasn't haute cuisine but it was a healthy, balanced meal with meat or fish and vegetables, followed by a piece of fruit or a yoghurt. At the Goldfields Primary School, however, the parents were expected to pack daily lunches for their children.

On Fridays, though, the school mums would provide a hot meal for all 35 children, giving my kids a nice break from their homemade sandwiches.

I was put in charge of organising the Friday lunch roster, which would've been a simple enough task had it not been for the interference of two type-A personalities on the parents' committee. One was Anita, Nathalie's mum, and the other was June, Nina's mum, both of whom just had way too much time on their hands. What made things worse was that they lived right next door to each other, and if my car was spotted outside one of their houses, I was sure to get a phonecall from the other, wanting details of what had been discussed. A lot of patience and diplomacy was needed to keep the interference to a minimum.

The Friday menu was varied. Depending on the ethnicity of the mother providing the meal, it could be a curry, samosas, rotis, fried rice, cassava fries, lasagne or spaghetti Bolognese. On those Fridays when no parent would be available for cooking duty, I'd organise a sausage sizzle, a cute name for a sausage on a bun, cooked on the barbecue by the headmaster or Mr Peters.

These Friday lunches would give me the opportunity to interact with all the children in the school. As I was setting up the tables, and putting out the cutlery and plates, they would come over to say hello or have a little chat. They were all so polite and fun to be around.

I also enjoyed volunteering with the reading. It was a time-consuming job that the teacher was glad to pass on to parent volunteers. While we listened to the kids read out loud, she could focus on teaching another group.

One Tuesday morning, I was just about to enter the classroom when a book suddenly came flying out of the window. I stopped dead in my tracks, ducking, as I wasn't sure how many more would follow.

I heard Mrs Peters' loud voice exclaim, 'I will not tolerate such messy and disgusting writing. Pauliasi, you must redo your homework, and this time try harder. I want to see neat handwriting.'

'Yes, miss,' came a young voice. 'May I go and retrieve my textbook?'

'Yes, you may.'

Pauliasi came running out and picked up his book, then looked at me and shrugged his shoulders as if to say, 'Watch out. She's not in a very good mood today,' and ran back inside.

Little Pauliasi didn't look the slightest bit perturbed about seeing his book fly out the window, and Melina never mentioned it that night either. In fact, she would always say how much she liked her teacher, and she was making enormous progress with her language skills. I assumed that books being flung outside was a common occurrence in Mrs Peters' class.

Two worlds

My father, Ken, was an English diplomat and was sent to France in the mid-1960s. He'd always told my brothers and me that it was a privilege to live abroad, and that we were guests in someone else's home country, and that we had to show respect at all times. He wouldn't tolerate any bad behaviour.

His words stayed with me, and I never considered myself above anyone. Ivan followed the same principles and treated everyone as equals.

But some Fijians seemed to accept the idea of white people's superiority. One day, when I was picking up Mansell from school, I asked his teacher, 'How was he today?'

'Very good,' she replied, cheerfully, 'but Bosso [meaning "boss"] didn't feel like doing any work today. He just played on the swings.'

'No, no, no!' I said, horrified. 'Miss Levatu, you are the teacher and this little boy has to listen to you.'

'Oh no, dear, it's okay.'

I was mortified. 'Please show me what work the other children did. I'll get Mansell to do it at home and he'll bring it to you tomorrow.'

That's exactly what we did, and in addition, I told little Mansell in no uncertain terms that he had to listen to his teacher, no matter what.

Expats around the world have a reputation of being condescending to the locals, snobby and arrogant. And, for the most part, I would agree with that description. Living in a foreign country can do weird things to some people's egos. It's even worse when the country is a developing country, and a good few expats start believing they're a class above the rest and pushing their weight around.

For example, I once saw Anita, another school mum, put on white gloves and go around her house with her maid, Talasi, by her side, checking if the dusting had been done to her liking. She lifted her finger, shoved it under Talasi's nose and yelled at her to start again. Talasi was a gentle old lady who certainly didn't deserve to be treated so badly.

When Ivan came home that evening and found me crying on the bed, I told him what had happened and how ashamed I felt of not having defended Talasi.

'I know how you feel,' he said. 'The injustice is really hard to take. You should've seen Emperor Gold Mine's previous owner, Jeffrey. He was in a league of his own. He really believed he was living in colonial times. I didn't witness this myself, but the story goes that a few squatters set up camp on some of the mine's leased land. They were asked to move but refused, so one morning Jeffrey came in on a white horse, leading a convoy of bulldozers through the camp.'

I listened, wide-eyed. 'And once, when Brad came down with the flu, Jeffrey called him and told him to come to his house at once. When Brad got there, Jeffrey asked him to remove his shoes and sit down. Then Jeffrey called in two male "servants" – as Jeffrey called them – and made them sit in front of Brad and massage his feet. Brad felt extremely uncomfortable and asked why. Jeffrey said it would draw out the illness.'

The thought of Brad, a big, burly ex rugby player, having his feet massaged by two men made me laugh.

'And you know, Allan, my boss?' Ivan went on. 'Well, he's always very stern with his staff. He always demands to be informed about every little thing before anyone makes a decision. One day a guy tripped and accidentally fell into the thickener tank. Before his colleagues would help him, they ran to Allan's office a few hundred metres down the road and waited patiently for Allan to see them, before asking if they could help their mate out. The poor guy was going round and round in the tank for a good thirty minutes before getting rescued!'

This wasn't as unbelievable as it sounds, and something happened to me that bore it out. When I was six months pregnant, I fell into a large pothole. It happened when I was shopping in Tavua one afternoon with Mansell. All I remember was not wanting to land on my stomach, so I twisted as I fell. I went all the way down, scraping my legs, arms and chin, which began bleeding. I immediately began shaking from head to foot as shock set in.

Although a large circle of people formed around me, nobody came forward to help. Poor little Mansell was crying, begging me to stand up. I finally picked myself up on my own, and we made our way back to the car.

Back home, after a strong cup of tea to help me calm down, I was able to make sense of why the locals had been so unhelpful. To them, I was a white lady who they'd been told to always show respect to, not a friend. They'd been confused and hesitant as to how to deal with the situation, which is why, although I'd seen genuine concern on their faces, nobody had helped. They'd been worried about consequences.

I didn't blame them. This fear of white authority was set deep in their culture, dating way back to when the first missionaries and colonials arrived. The locals had endured the preaching, and eventually had had to relinquish their culture, land and resources through conflicts with the western imperial and capital representatives.

▲ ▲ ▲

The video store in Tavua was run by the lovely Rajni. She was always there, no matter the time of day. She loved our kids and found it very cute the way they'd go and position themselves in front of the TV, miming the dance moves of the Bollywood movie that was always playing.

She was forever trying to get me to rent one, but I resisted. Call me a meanie, but I didn't think I could handle that music blasting through my house from morning till night – and that's what would have happened, because my children wouldn't have let me turn it off. I understood the fascination: there were so many bright colours, the choreography was entertaining, and the characters were dramatic and lively.

The first time Ivan came home with a rented video, I found it a surreal viewing experience. I heard a sneeze but couldn't match it with anyone on the screen; then someone laughed, but I hadn't seen anyone in the movie laugh – and anyway, it didn't make sense, because we were watching a dramatic scene. Where were these noises coming from?

Then I saw the silhouette of a person standing up in the foreground, and it all suddenly came clear. Someone was filming the movie from his theatre chair! It was a pirated copy.

This was, of course, illegal everywhere else in the world, but in Fiji, it was a way of life and how you got your entertainment. Movies that had only just been released in theatres were available within a week there, as long as you didn't mind that some of the recordings weren't the best. They only cost a dollar a movie from Rajni's store, no big deal.

During quiet times, I would leave the kids a little longer in front of their show while Rajni and I caught up. She was my closest Indo-Fijian friend and I loved listening to her stories. She'd only recently married and lived in her in-laws' house with other siblings and spouses, twelve people in total. Being the newest member of her husband's family, most of the chores fell to her. She was responsible for making dinner, even if she was working twelve hours a day at the store, so she would get up at 5 am to do all the meal prep, and on arriving home in the evenings, jump straight into the kitchen. What a tough life.

She often told me how she dreamt of having her own home, just for herself and her husband, although she knew it was going to be several years before they would have enough money saved even for just a down payment.

She was grateful for her kind husband. Her father had arranged her marriage and she acknowledged the fact that she'd snagged a good one. She told me about many of her friends who were caught in loveless marriages, and how several had taken their own lives, as they had no other way out. 'I was lucky,' she explained. 'My father tried to match me with a boy who had similar interests and the same views as me. I can't say it was love at first sight, but we became friends and then I fell in love with him. He was very gentle on our first night, and I liked him even more for it.'

I thanked my lucky stars for being born in a country where I could decide who my life partner would be.

It was hard for me to understand her life and culture, but I loved our chats, opening my mind to the outside world. I was sorry to hear about her struggles at home: her mother-in-law was a difficult person, never satisfied no matter how hard Rajni tried to please her.

Listening to her made me compare my and my friends' situation to hers, and I felt ashamed of all the times we complained about silly little things.

School plays and outings

Fiji became an independent sovereign state on 10 October 1970, and the day was an annual national holiday, with festivities and parties organised from the capital, Suva, right down to the smallest remote mountain village.

In our first year in Fiji, our little Goldfields Primary School was putting on a concert to commemorate the anniversary of this historic day, and Melina was very excited about taking part. She didn't reveal what her class was planning – she told us, with a very serious face, 'It's a secret. We can't talk about it. You'll just have to wait.'

The big night finally arrived, and we were treated to the sight of the children in beautiful costumes. The boys wore grass skirts, shell necklaces on their bare chests, armbands made of green leaves, and tattoo-like designs on their upper arms; each held a spear or a tribal war club. The girls wore dresses or skirts of tapa (a traditional cloth made from the inner bark of the mulberry or fig tree), with a hibiscus or frangipani flower behind their left ear, indicating their unmarried status.

The evening started with everyone standing for the singing of Fiji's national anthem; Fijians have beautiful voices, and it was very emotional listening to their harmonious singing. The chorus is joyful, fun and easy to remember, and I often found myself singing or humming it: 'For Fiji, ever Fiji, let our voices ring with pride. For Fiji, ever Fiji, her name hail far and wide!'

After a short introduction, it was time for Melina and her classmates to give us a traditional dance. This little troupe was dressed in grass skirts and white T-shirts, with frangipani-flower leis around their necks and on their heads. As they swayed, barefoot, to the sound of island music, I cried my eyes out with pride, watching my little girl beaming, performing with her friends in front of a cheerful audience. It was hard to believe that only six weeks before she didn't even know where Fiji was.

Then came Mr Peters, to recount the story of the ill-fated Thomas Baker. You could have heard a pin drop: with his warm, deep, powerful voice and emotive gestures, he had a way of captivating his audience. We all hung on his words.

'Thomas Baker was an Australian Methodist missionary. He arrived in Fiji with his wife and lived on the coast. He would spend his days preaching, trying to convert the "heathens". His three daughters were born in Fiji, and he was highly regarded among the local communities. Years later, the Baker family decided to return to Australia for good, but Thomas was determined to make one last trip, deep into the interior of Viti Levu to reach the most remote mountainous tribes of the island. There were still tensions between the white man and tribe leaders, and many warned him against making the trip. But he was determined and confident that God Almighty would protect him.

'So he set off with eight followers on this perilous journey. He arrived in the village of Navatusila late at night, not to a warm welcome, as he had envisioned, but to a more reserved and tense greeting. He and his men were given some food and were allowed to sleep there.

'The next morning, he noticed that the chief was wearing his comb. He was disgusted: he thought of these natives as heathens, not yet converted to Christianity, and regarded their big mops of hair as unclean. In anger, he reached into the chief's hair and pulled out the comb.'

At this crucial point in the story, Mr Peters' voice hit a crescendo, and then he fell silent. We all held our breath: what was going to happen?

'Nobody is allowed to touch a chief's head! It is sacrilege!' Mr Peters suddenly shouted. Everyone jumped.

'As the chief shouted for his men to seize Thomas Baker and his entourage, the reverend and his friends ran as fast as they could, trying to escape – but alas, they were caught and clubbed to death.'

Mr Peters allowed another silence, while we all contemplated this gruesome end. 'The bodies were brought back to the chief, so he could see for himself that the ultimate punishment had been exacted. The chief took one look at the bloodied bodies and yelled, "Let's cook them and eat them!"'

And on that final note, Mr Peters rose and took a bow. The audience erupted in applause and cheers.

As much as I'd loved the telling of the story, I recalled the sign in the butcher shop that I'd seen that first day – 'white people is better than corned beef' – and decided then and there never to touch a Fijian's head.

▲ ▲ ▲

Melina, my little island girl, prepares for her group's traditional dance display.

Although Mansell wasn't in the school play, he got into the spirit of things with a frangipani lei and crown.

Mansell's preschool was organising a field trip to the private beach that Emperor Gold Mines owned a short distance out of town. His teacher approached me one afternoon when I was picking him up and invited me to join the outing. I was very grateful and thanked her for the opportunity to tag along.

So early one Wednesday morning I pitched up at the school with a backpack full of necessities, including sunscreen, towels, mosquito repellent, hats and sunglasses, and a picnic basket filled with fruit, sandwiches and plenty of water.

'You didn't need to bring all that,' said Miss Levatu, after giving me a big hug. 'My assistant, Vasiti, and I have enough food to feed an army!'

Three other school mums were taking part in this outing, including Marianna's mum, Susana. I'd seen her and her husband at the primary school during the Fiji Day presentation, and someone had told us that he was a ratu (chief), a noble rank inherited by succession, who had aspirations of one day maybe trying to run for president.

We heard the bus coming up the hill before we saw it: it sounded as if it was stuck in first gear, and as it came over the rise, we saw a dark cloud of smoke belching out of its exhaust pipe. It certainly didn't sound very roadworthy, and I had my doubts about its reliability. But I seemed to be the only one worried, as the kids and teachers took off running in its direction, welcoming it with a loud cheer. It was quite a sight. The bus was painted in colourful Indian designs, and the interior was adorned with tassels and bells, adding to the joyful cacophony.

We all piled in. Mansell wanted to sit with his friend Tomasi, so I sat by the open window, enjoying the view. As we bounced along, I was once again humbled by the privilege of experiencing such amazing adventures. When we go on holiday to exotic locations, we might get to see a small part of how other people live, but this was so much more. We'd been given the opportunity to be part of the locals' lives and make friendships that would last a lifetime. Most of all, I thought of the kids and how enriching this was for them.

As we neared the beach, the kids all leapt up off their seats, pointing at the water. They were so excited and so was I – I'd spent many holidays on the Mediterranean Sea, but this was so different. Tall coconut palms lined a pristine white beach, and the ocean lapped the shore in multiple shades of blue, turquoise and green. It all looked like a stunning postcard.

We set up the picnic area, then organised the kids, making sure they all had their flotation devices on, as well as sunscreen. Then we all headed down to the water's edge. As I put my feet in, I was surprised at how warm it was – the Med, even on the hottest day of summer, might be about 25 degrees Celsius, but this was closer to 30. My kind of temperature!

We built sandcastles, collected seashells and watched hermit crabs. By noon, we were all ravenous, and headed back to the shaded area to grab some lunch. The kindergarten's kitchen staff had prepared chicken curry, rice and chickpeas, and I felt quite embarrassed about my two ham-and-cheese sandwiches.

'Please help yourself,' said Susana. She was so friendly and welcoming, I instantly took to her, she told me that she and Miss Levatu had known each other since they were little and had gone to the same school as kids. Susanna called Miss Levatu 'Biscuit', and I asked if that was her first name.

Susana laughed. 'No. She's from the island of Rotuma, and the legend goes that when the natives first met the Europeans back in the 19th century, they were offered some dry biscuits. The locals liked them so much that they planted them, thinking they would grow. They did swell, at first, from the water they absorbed, so they initially thought they'd succeeded in growing a biscuit tree.'

Miss Levatu told me that the other nickname her people got was 'Buttons', because when a sailor once gave a Rotuman woman some coins, she cursed him, thinking he was trying to trick her with bad buttons which had no holes in them to sew.

Chatting and laughing, Susana handed me a large plate of the delicious-smelling curry but was quick to warn me about the birds that were circling above us. 'The Myna birds are as disruptive and annoying as pigeons and gulls, always on the lookout for food and on the attack as soon as you sit a plate down. They're not native to here, you see; they were introduced in the late 1800s to control pests in the sugarcane crops but they've now become the worst invasive species, and are a threat to the native and much prettier birds.'

'That's a real shame,' I said, deciding to keep a watchful eye on my food.

I admired the way the women ate their food, using only their fingers. They made it look so easy, first taking some rice, then scooping up the chicken without spilling a drop of juice. When I tried, the juice dripped down my fingers and ran up my arms. I was a complete mess.

The irony of the situation wasn't lost on me, and it brought a smile to my face, comparing this meal to the ones I'd been forced to endure as a child. In France meals can go on for hours, and then there's also the complicated table etiquette: the order in which to use your cutlery and glasses; never to eat the bread before the first course has been served; always to use your knife and fork, however tempting it might be to pick up a fry with your fingers and pop it in your mouth; keeping your hands above the table but no elbows on the table.

'Mum, what are you doing?' Mansell asked, shocked. 'You're always telling Melina and me to eat properly, with our knives and forks, and look at you!'

Seeing the horror on my little boy's face, I realised that I must have passed on quite a bit of that complicated upbringing to my own children.

'Wait till I tell Dad and Melina tonight!' Mansell added, then he had a fit of the giggles that he couldn't stop.

I apologised to the women about my poor eating style, but they just laughed and handed me bunches of serviettes, encouraging me and giving me tips on how to master this new concept.

Then it was time for dessert. The women cut up some green mangoes, then brought out a container of salt and another of chilli powder. 'Take a wedge, and dip it in chilli powder, then in salt,' Susana instructed. 'Here, try it. What do you think?'

I couldn't answer because the chilli-laced fruit had awakened all my tastebuds at once. The acidity from the green mango mixed with the spice and the salt exploded in my mouth, and the next minute I was coughing and sneezing, my eyes were watering, and my face was as red as a tomato. I gulped down some water and tried to catch my breath.

'I am so sorry,' Susana said. 'I didn't mean to almost kill you!'

'It's okay. I actually quite like it,' I said, as I recovered, and then helped myself to more. I really did enjoy it.

'You know,' said Miss Levatu, casually, 'we have the belief that when a woman craves this, it means she's pregnant.'

While we finished packing and tidying up, Vasiti took the kids for a last walk along the beach. They suddenly all pointed to something in the water, jumping up and down, and we came running to see what the fuss was about. There was a long black and white sea snake swimming just a few metres offshore. I'd never seen anything like it before but, judging by the frantic shouts from one of the mums and Vasiti, I gathered it wasn't something you wanted to encounter while in the water.

I told Ivan about our sighting that evening and he confirmed they're venomous but noted that as their mouths are tiny, they rarely get to bite humans.

Reunited with our belongings

Three months after our arrival, we finally got word that the ship had arrived in the port of Lautoka and that our container was making its final journey to us by truck. The company sent a crew in that morning to remove the temporary furniture, and when our own belongings arrived, the movers worked quickly and efficiently to get our furniture set up and the boxes neatly stacked out of the way.

As I was opening a box labelled 'kitchen utensils', a sudden wave of homesickness swept over me. There was a half-eaten, dried-up croissant, and I remembered the day the French company had come to pack us up and one of the workers had looked everywhere for his misplaced morning snack. And here it was! It had travelled halfway around the world.

I was surprised at the emotions I was feeling over a half-eaten baked good. I suddenly longed to be able to pop out for a chocolate croissant from the little pastry shop down the main street, bumping into friends along the way, chatting and laughing over silly things.

I was quickly brought back to reality by two men carrying in one of the couches and wanting instructions as to where it went. It was a couch that Ivan had originally bought here in Fiji when he'd first worked here four years before, and I smiled, realising that some of these things had actually done a complete round trip.

This particular couch set was made from palmwood. The company that made it, called Pacific Green, had opened its first factory in the 1980s just outside Sigatoka, a town on the south coast of the main island. They used plantation coconut palms to create long-lasting one-of-a-kind hardwood pieces via an environmentally friendly process.

Melita and I worked all day getting the house back in order, and by the time Ivan came through the door that evening, I was exhausted.

He was excited to be reunited with his belongings, especially his guitar and his books. He came into the kitchen brandishing a funny-looking item. A long piece of wood with a metal claw at one end, it resembled a heavy-duty backscratcher.

'Love, you rest,' he said. 'I'm going to make you an authentic Fijian coconut-milk curry for dinner.'

'And what are you doing with that backscratcher?' I asked.

'It's a sakarau, a coconut grater. I'm going to get a coconut from our garden, and I'll show you how the Fijian women extract the creamy milk from it.'

I was excited to watch the process, but then began having doubts when Ivan struggled for at least twenty minutes just trying to get the outer husk off the coconut. Mick came over to help, bringing a hammer and some screwdrivers, and they eventually managed to remove the husk – only to find that the coconut was rotten, and they had to start all over again. But a good forty minutes later, Ivan was finally holding two pieces of nice white coconut.

We headed indoors, where the demonstration would take place in the lounge. He placed the contraption on a chair, then sat on the wooden flat handle with the claw facing him and started scraping the coconut against it. Pieces of the grated fruit fell into a bowl positioned on the floor. It was clearly quite a strenuous exercise and Ivan began sweating profusely.

As it was getting late, I surreptitiously slipped into the kitchen and quietly put on a Bolognese sauce, just in case my darling's plans didn't come to fruition.

Back in the lounge, he was looking quite despondent at the result of his tremendous efforts. There was only the equivalent of a cup or so of shredded coconut in the bowl. 'Now all I have to do is squeeze the shreds, and this will give us the creamy liquid needed for dinner,' he said, sounding more confident than he looked.

But as much as he squeezed and pressed, he managed to get only two drops out of the coconut – and they were a very unappetising black in colour, as his hands were dirty from the husk.

Little Mansell, who'd been watching intently, said, 'Daddy, I thought you said you were making milk. Where is it, Daddy?'

'Well, son, I'm not sure where I went wrong,' Ivan conceded, and suddenly we were all rolling around on the floor, laughing hysterically. He might not have provided dinner, but the entertainment had been amazing.

We never gave the sakarau another try, but I always smile when I pick up a can of coconut milk in the stores.

▲ ▲ ▲

A couple of weeks later, another move was in the offing: our permanent house was finally ready.

Melita and I repacked all our belongings into the boxes, then settled down to wait for the local truck and guys to arrive. I'd been told to expect them by 9 am but it was now 10:30 and we were still waiting.

I called Ivan to see if he could hurry things along from his end. 'The truck was being cleaned after completing the garbage pickup,' he said.

'What do you mean, the garbage pickup?' I asked, hoping that I'd misunderstood.

'They're scheduled to move us after the garbage pickup, but don't worry, they're probably late cause they're giving the truck an extra scrub.'

They finally showed up and I decided not to inspect the inside of the truck too closely. I did give my belongings a bit of a sniff once they got to our new home, but there was no food residue or weird smells, so I was quite content.

We now were living on the other side of the mine, closer to the primary school, across from the bowling club and fifty metres from Melita's village. The house was built on the side of a lush hill, overlooking the mill and helipad. It was very spacious, with three large bedrooms, a big lounge, a nice-sized kitchen and bathroom, and – the best feature – a huge deck with 180-degree views of the tropical surroundings. The laundry room was in a shed at the front of the house.

The children were happy because their friends lived just down the street, so they could socialise easily after school.

▲ ▲ ▲

Me sitting with our dog, Shadow, in the garden of our home,
which overlooked the mine. It had pawpaws, mangoes, bananas,
coconuts and even an avocado tree, and my favourite, frangipani trees.

An issue that I had to work through was the realisation that I would probably never live in my home country again, as Salsigne was the last gold mine in operation in France, making Ivan's work prospects there very slim.

During those first few months in Fiji, I was constantly comparing my new life with my old one, thinking about my family, my friends, food I was craving, the familiar TV shows and French music. I felt as if I was a newborn adult, having to learn everything from scratch, from simple things like driving on the left side of the road to making new friends, learning about a new culture, and even, to some degree, learning a new language. My spoken English was okay, but I still had some mishaps, like the time I upset an Australian woman without meaning to because I mistakenly used the wrong word.

It happened when a group of women and I were sitting at a table at the golf club, and one of them, Trish, was telling us how she and her husband were heading to Noosa the following week.

It wasn't the first time I'd heard that name, so I piped up, 'Oh, Noosa seems like a very common destination.'

Trish turned to me with a look of irritated disgust on her face and snapped, 'There is nothing common about Noosa,' before marching off to join her husband at another table.

I felt terrible. The French word *commun* means 'popular', which is what I'd meant. And to be fair to Trish, there really was nothing common about Noosa, which is a beautiful resort town on the Sunshine Coast of Queensland, Australia. So I get why Trish thought I was just being snobbish.

I felt miserable on the drive home, and no sooner was I in the house than I burst into tears. After managing to calm me down,

Ivan listened as I explained my faux pas, then he gave me a big hug. 'Poor love, you didn't deserve that,' he said, soothingly. 'Trish is way too sensitive. It is kind of funny, though.'

'I don't think so. I felt really stupid,' I muttered.

'You're speaking a foreign language! There's nothing stupid about that! Next time, tell her to speak French and see how she gets on.'

My darling husband was trying to make me feel good and protecting me, and his kind words and humour did lift my spirits, but I made a promise to myself that from that day on, I was going to read only English books. I immediately picked up one of Ivan's favourites, Ken Follett's *Pillars of the Earth*. It was a thick book with small print, and it took me a good two months to finish it, but I persevered. It felt good to realise my English was improving.

As for the homesickness, time heals, or maybe the memories just fade. You do gradually come to terms with your new reality. You get to a point where you can laugh at yourself and your national quirks, customs and mannerisms.

Some years before, one of our hotel guests had left me the memoir *A Year in Provence* by Peter Mayle, an Englishman who'd moved to France and later wrote about his trials and tribulations while interacting with French tradesmen during his house renovations. The first time I tried reading it, I saw his words as insults, and became so offended that I threw the book in the bin. Now, reading Ivan's copy, I thoroughly enjoyed it. I could appreciate my country and its people's originality from an outsider's point of view, and it made me laugh and proud all at once.

Another toxic thought going around and around in my head

was that I was now a miner's wife, and for some reason the image I had in my brain was of an obese, greasy-haired, foul-mouthed, tattoos-and-sweatpants woman. It wasn't what I looked like but I feared I might turn into it.

The person who helped me through my mental struggle was my dear Judy – also, incidentally, a miner's wife, and who didn't look anything like my horrible mental image either.

'Don't be so silly,' she said, when I admitted my fear. 'Who here do you know who looks like that?'

I thought for a few moments, then admitted, 'Well, nobody.'

'So where do you get that picture from?'

'I saw a woman like that on the news once, I think.'

By this stage, Judy was laughing out loud at me. 'Forget that nonsense!' she said. 'What I will do, though, is give you some advice on how to navigate as a couple through this world.'

I was instantly all ears.

'Mining, as you can see, is a question of being always on the road, which isn't ideal for a family, and always in small towns – your chances of living in Sydney, Brisbane or Perth are remote. So, given that, you have two options. The first is living like you are here, together with your husband. It can be either on the mine site or in a mining town, which are usually nice but in the middle of nowhere. Kalgoorlie, for instance.'

When I looked puzzled, Judy explained, 'It's like the queen of all mining towns in Australia. It has a population of roughly 35 000 people, and all the amenities you could wish for. I'm sure you'll end up there at some point during Ivan's career. The only catch is that it's seven hours' drive inland from Perth.'

'Ah, yes, as you said – remote,' I said, and she nodded. 'So what's my second option?'

'It's called fly-in-and-out, and what it means is that you and the kids would be based in a large city, Perth, for instance. Ivan would fly out to the mine for two, three weeks at a time, and then come home for a week to ten days.'

'That doesn't sound great.'

'It's not. It's very hard on a relationship. Your husband flies off to work, and you and your kids settle into a routine that doesn't include him. You have to keep living while he's away, so you see your friends, you pursue your interests, you manage the house, the kids. You're in charge of everything. Then, suddenly, he's back. He thinks that because he's home, you should drop everything and just look after him, or do things just with him, and forget your girl-friends. He might treat the house like a hotel, which wouldn't be his fault, as he would have no chores to do at the mine site, so it would be easy for him to forget that at home there are no maids. These are little things, but slowly, you find yourself resenting him. Don't get me wrong, you're always super happy to see each other, but over time, the disruption starts weighing on your relationship.'

Wondering if Judy was talking from experience, I said, 'Looking at you and Mick together, I can't imagine your marriage ever being in trouble. You look so happy.'

'We are now, but we've had our struggles, like most couples. The time Mick worked away was one of those difficult times. So, in short, my advice to you is to go where your husband goes.'

I never forgot those words, and so far, Ivan and I have lived by this rule.

Bad hair days and weekends away

The one thing that suffered tremendously from life in the tropics was my hair. The humidity either sent it into a complete frizz or it sat flat as a pancake on my face. So, after two months of battling with it, I decide to consult with June about who she trusted with her hair. Caucasian hair is very different from indigenous or Indian hair, so we couldn't just walk into any salon and get a hair treatment or a cut.

June told me that a hairdresser, Oscar, came up from Lautoka, one of the bigger cities, an hour away, once every few weeks and saw his expat clients at the Tavua Hotel. I made an appointment and waited with excitement for the big day. Would I have highlights done? What kind of cut would I get this time? It would be nice to get a blow-dry and look smart for a change.

I was greeted in the hotel reception and taken to the hair salon – which wasn't at all what I'd expected. It was a backpackers' room with a muddy floor, furnished with three bunkbeds (unmade) and a chair crammed in the corner in front of a tiny mirror. It smelled of stale sweat and stinky feet. Never mind, I thought to myself, I'm not here to spend the night but to get pampered.

I could hear some noise in the bathroom, which was a small,

windowless room tacked on the back of the backpackers' room, and, peeping inside, I saw a woman bent over with her head under a shower while a man – Oscar, as it turned out – rinsed her hair. I introduce myself and Oscar gave me a big smile and a 'Bula vinaka'. He told me to grab a seat while he finished up with his client.

When it was my turn, he assessed my hair situation with a frown on his face that didn't inspire much confidence. He finally let out a huge sigh and said, 'Honey, there's not much I can do with this.'

'That bad, huh?' I said, dispirited.

'The only solution is a perm,' he stated.

I looked at him in complete shock. Didn't perms go out of style in the 1980s? But apparently the humidity had fried a few of my neurons, because the words I heard come out of my mouth were 'If you say so ....'

'Honey, you need the volume. Trust me, you're going to look gorgeous.'

So I sat through the archaic process of getting my hair permed, and finally Oscar led me into the bathroom and bent me awkwardly into the shower, rinsing my hair and yelling enthusiastically, 'Oh, yes! I like it!'

Then the lights went out.

Working in complete darkness in the tiny windowless room, Oscar managed to drench me almost from head to toe, so by the time I regained my seat in front of the mirror, I was totally drenched and my hair looked like it had shrunk as well as been fried.

Oscar went off to find out how long the power outage was

intended to last and came back with a grim look. 'Honey, I'm really sorry but apparently there's been a major blow-up at the power station, so it looks like it's off for the rest of the day. But don't worry, just let your hair air-dry and it'll look amazing. You won't have to do anything with it! You'll just have beautiful volume and curls.'

I had my doubts and sure enough, as my hair dried on the drive home, I looked more and more like a poodle, with a tight frizz rather than beautiful loose curls.

As I stepped through the front door at home, the kids came running up to greet me, then stopped dead. Mansell quickly hid behind Melina, and both just stared at me.

Melina was the first to speak. 'What happened to your hair?' she asked in a small voice.

I was determined to make the best of it. Giving a twirl, I said, 'I got a perm. Do you like it?'

'You look like Vanille!' Mansell blurted out. He'd nailed it: Vanille had been the toy poodle we'd had in France.

When Ivan got home from work and got a look at my new hairstyle, he didn't comment but turned and walked quickly into the bedroom, not able to hide the smile on his face. I'd always complained about the lack of reaction and comments I got from my family when I came back from hairdressers in the past but not this time.

Yes, I felt like crying when I looked at my hair, but at the same time I laughed my head off looking back at the few hours I'd spent in that backpackers' room. I'd actually enjoyed the experience, despite the outcome.

A few months later, with the perm finally growing out, I decided to visit a hair salon at one of the best resorts in Fiji during one of our weekend getaways. I had the brilliant idea that rich American tourists would want to get their hair done after a few days in the sea, so the hairstylist would be used to Caucasian hair. Leaving my family enjoying their relaxing time by the pool, I went to get pampered. This time, I wanted some blonde highlights in my naturally very dark hair.

Mariana, the charming and welcoming hairstylist, said the highlights would be no problem. 'And let's do another perm at the same time – you'll look like your old self in no time,' she added.

Unbelievably, I hadn't learnt my lesson about staying away from perms, maybe because this time I was in a proper salon, with real washbasins and fancy chairs. Within a few minutes I was sitting with my hair all up in rollers, waiting for the chemicals to turn my hair back into poodle pelt. In the meantime, Mariana showed me a few swatches of blonde to choose from.

The perm chemicals rinsed out and my hair dried, the time came for the torture of the highlights: Mariana squeezed a tight-fitting cap with tiny holes over my head, and, using an instrument that resembled a crochet hook, pulled through a good number of strands. With the hair that was to remain my natural dark colour covered and protected by the cap, Mariana slathered the pulled-through tresses with the colour chemicals, then looked at her watch and said, 'We'll leave that on for—'

I realised she was staring in astonishment at my hair, so I looked too, and realised, to my horror, that it had started to smoke. 'Is this normal?' I asked, in as calm a voice as I could muster.

'Oh, my goodness! Oh, my goodness!' Mariana shouted, then ran out the door.

She returned with her supervisor, who could hardly stop herself from laughing. 'Get it off quick!' she shouted.

Some washes and a deep-condition later, I was back in the chair, while we all assessed the damage. Not only was my hair burnt to a crisp, the colour, not having had enough time to properly bleach the pulled-through strands, was bright orange.

I was beyond having a sense of humour about it and, in tears, I rejoined my obliviously happy little family at the pool. The kids took one look at me and paddled away, leaving Dad to deal with what looked like a very upset mummy.

'It doesn't look too bad, love,' my husband said, soothingly.

'Take your sunglasses off.'

He did, then quickly put them back on. 'Okay, I see what you mean,' he conceded, and added, 'Never mind, I still love you.'

The bad-hair saga would eventually give us lots of fun stories and photos to look back on and laugh about.

Just not that day.

▲ ▲ ▲

We were one of the few expat families who didn't have a pool at home, so on weekends when Ivan wasn't on call, we'd head down to Nadi for a night or two. Located on the west coast, it's one of Fiji's largest cities and, due to its proximity to the airport, is also a tourist hub. We were very lucky to benefit from local rates at the beach resorts, which were cheaper by forty percent compared to tourist rates.

We usually went on a Saturday morning, popping in at the American store en route to pick up a few treats that were impossible to find anywhere else – caramel popcorn, peanut butter, bagels, cream cheese and the kids' bubblegum-flavoured toothpaste. Then we'd stop off for lunch at Chefs, a restaurant with items on its menu that you couldn't find anywhere else. The kids loved their Mac and cheese, while Ivan and I usually went for either duck confit or lamb chops.

After lunch, we'd hunt the stores for clothes that might fit our kids. Melina was lucky enough to get hand-me-downs from older kids in Vatukoula, but poor thin little Mansell wasn't as fortunate, as our friends' children were all older. Our best option was to buy him touristy T-shirts and shorts, with big Mickey Mouses or Donald Ducks and 'Bula Fiji' written all over them. Luckily, he seemed not to mind.

We'd given up on finding shoes to fit any of us, as Fijians have big and wide feet, whereas the Indians had narrow and small ones.

Once, we visited the golf shop, where Ivan was determined to deck me out with my personal set of clubs (I'd been borrowing a set up to that point). The sales assistant was extremely knowledgeable, and as we were leaving, Ivan gave him an open invitation to Vatukoula's golf course, thinking that he probably got very few chances to play a game. We felt quite stupid a few days later when we found out he was Vijay Singh's brother, so probably not only extremely good at the game, but with access to the most prestigious golf clubs in the country. We never did see him in our neck of the woods.

By mid-afternoon, we'd be lazing around the pool. Melina,

who'd always been afraid of water although she knew how to swim, would usually be reluctant to go further than knee deep, but Ivan and I had noticed her getting braver all the time. Although Mansell loved the water and could swim, he still asked to have the belt on before heading in. We kept telling him he didn't need it, but it was psychological and made him feel protected.

By 6 pm we'd be lined up on the beach, Ivan and me holding our favourite cocktails and the kids with fruit punches, waiting for the daily magical moment of watching the sun drop into the ocean and the sky light up in beautiful shades of orange, pink and purple. People clapped and cheered when it happened, and it was always a happy moment shared with a group of total strangers witnessing the beauty of life.

Dinner was a fun time, as the Fijians loved children and always came to interact with the kids, showing them magic tricks, bringing them treats or taking them into the kitchen for an ice cream.

Ivan and I enjoyed watching them so at ease in their new surroundings. We noticed that Mansell had even developed a bit of an island accent when he spoke English, and I overheard him say to a little boy he was playing with in the pool that he was Fijian.

Melina, Mansell and me at Warwick Resort on the main island of
Viti Levu in January 1997.

Melina at sunset at the Sheraton Fiji resort on Denarau Island,
which is accessible via a short causeway from Nadi.

Christmas time

With only a few weeks to go until Christmas, I had nothing organised. Part of the reason was that I just couldn't believe that Christmas was around the corner – where was the snow, the cold temperatures, the winter coats, the cozy nights by the fire?

To the contrary, we were going through the hottest time of the year, with sweltering temperatures and a hundred per cent humidity forcing us to spend most of our days inside by the air conditioner. Also, of course, we lived in a very remote area, so we weren't constantly reminded of this festive time of the year by glittery shop windows all decked out with Santas, elves and Christmas trees.

Tavua, our closest town, was geared for covering just the basics, and there was nothing there worthy of a Christmas gift. So we made a trip down to Lautoka, where we were able to pick up a Christmas tree – the saddest-looking wobbly artificial tree I'd ever seen, with a few flimsy branches sparsely covered in bright green tinsel. We picked up some gold tinsel to wrap around it and a few balls to complete the look.

The kids were very excited, completely oblivious to the tackiness of the tree: they just loved the meaning, that Santa was coming very soon.

Finding the perfect Christmas gift for each of them was much more difficult. Ivan and I hunted high and low in both Lautoka and Nadi but had to eventually come to terms with the fact that quality toys simply were not to be had in Fiji, period. All that was available were cheap copies of Barbies and Batman figurines.

I wanted to extra-spoil the kids this Christmas, due to the massive upheaval we'd put them through. Of course, I was projecting my own feelings on them – the guilt I felt for foisting a complete life change on them – because the truth was that they were fine. They hadn't shown any signs of distress – which, paradoxically, made me want to reward them even more, for being such great sports.

I was getting really worked up because I couldn't seem to find a purchase worthy of the effort they'd put in, when Ivan fortunately painted the bigger picture for me. 'Listen, Fiona,' he said, waiting for me to wipe away my tears, and then gently taking my hands, 'kids don't think like us adults. Their thought processes are much purer and simpler. For them, it's Christmas, and Santa is going to bring them a gift. They don't look at the monetary value of the gift; they just want a toy, a surprise, and that's what they're going to get.' Then he added something I hadn't thought of before. 'Besides, they're not getting bombarded by advertisements for the must-have toy of the season.'

'You're right,' I said. 'I have no clue what that is this year.'

'And neither do they,' he said with a wink. 'We just have to surprise them, and they'll be happy. Trust me.'

And, of course, he was right. Mansell got a huge shiny red remote-controlled car with big headlights, wheels and mirrors, which did all kind of tricks, spinning, drifting and bouncing off the walls, and he was a happy boy. And Melina got a fake Barbie doll but was most excited about the bunch of bangles and hair accessories that I'd picked up at our local Indian store.

▲ ▲ ▲

A few days before Christmas, as we were walking along a shopping street, Mansell noticed someone he thought he recognised. Stopping short, he tugged at my hand and asked, 'Mummy, who's that?'

On the other side of the street was a person in full Santa regalia, standing and ringing a bell. Sweating profusely, he was shouting out, 'Ho, ho, ho! Who wants to sit on Santa's lap?'

'He's black and I know Santa isn't black,' Mansell pointed out.

'Ah, that's Santa's helper,' I told my confused son. 'You know Santa lives in the North Pole, and Fiji is very far from there, so to make sure all children get spoilt on Christmas Day, Santa asks his most trusted helpers to lend a hand. Let's go over and see him.'

'I don't think I want to,' Mansell said, holding my hand more tightly.

'Well,' I said, 'you wouldn't want Santa to drop your gift at the wrong address, would you? Remember, we don't live in Carcassonne any more, and someone has to tell him that.'

'Oh yes, you're right. I'd better go and tell him that Melina and I live here now, and he can pass the message on to Santa.'

So my little shy boy marched over and told 'Santa's helper' all about his move to Fiji, and got confirmation that he would make sure that Santa came to visit him and his sister on Christmas eve.

▲ ▲ ▲

The processing-plant Christmas party was a celebration everyone looked forward to. It was time to celebrate the accomplishments, the hard work and sacrifices that had gone into making the company profitable, safe and a good place to work. For the eclectic management team of over a hundred people – mainly Fijians, and including metallurgists, electricians, foremen and secretaries – it was an opportunity to share a good time with their spouses, for everyone to mingle and let their hair down in a fun and jovial atmosphere.

The party was held at the bowling club, across the street from our house. From the early afternoon, we could smell the lovo. This traditional technique of cooking meat, fish and vegetables starts with digging a pit in the ground, then adding some hot coals before putting the food on top. Everything is then covered with banana leaves, soil or potato sacks, and it's left to slowly cook over a few hours. The party was to start at around 6 pm.

Ivan helped me pick out an outfit, and we agreed on a long flowy summer dress, while he wore shorts and a bula shirt, which is a colourful shirt with tribal patterns and flowers on it.

The clubhouse had been scrubbed and decorated for the event, and it looked amazing. Colourful garlands were hung across the walls and ceiling, and cheerful Christmas songs played on the stereo. A huge dance floor was cleared in the middle of the room, and a buffet was set up on tables in the far corner.

It was nice to see everyone all dressed up, with the women as well as the men wearing a flower behind their ear – the left to denote single status, the right for married people. In the olden days, a flower behind each ear denoted commoners, while those with chiefly titles would wear just the one.

Laughter and dancing were the main objective that evening, and I hardly saw Ivan, as he was solicited by everyone for a dance. In Fiji it was quite normal for two men to dance together, holding hands, with no sexual connotation.

I enjoyed watching Fijians with their inherent natural rhythm dance, the swaying and moving to the music being mesmerising. They hardly moved their feet but undulated their whole bodies from the ground up. They made it look so natural and effortless. It just didn't look the same when I tried, and looking at Ivan, I could see he was experiencing the same struggles. It didn't stop any of us from having a fantastic time, though.

The food was very tasty, and included my first time trying palusami, a traditional Fijian and Samoan dish made of corned beef, onion, garlic and coconut cream, wrapped in taro leaves and cooked in the lovo. One of the cooks told me how careful they had to be to ensure the taro leaves were properly cooked, as they're poisonous when eaten raw.

The party went on well into the night, and at one stage we all stood up, held hands and sang the Fijian national anthem, swaying from side to side.

I was so grateful for the opportunity of meeting such beautiful people, enjoying their culture and food with them, and making memories I would treasure for the rest of my life.

▲ ▲ ▲

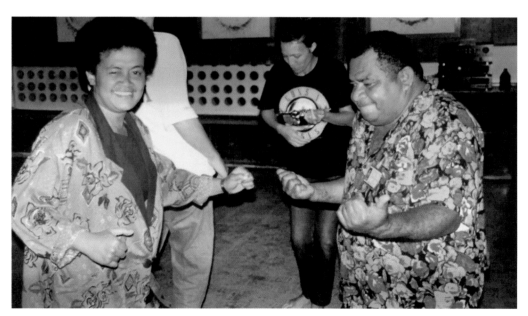

Fun with friends at the company Christmas party.

101

It was a few days after Christmas, and the kids were still on summer break, enjoying visiting their friends, riding their bikes and walking down to the corner shop for ice cream.

We headed over to June's house for the kids to play with their friends Nina and Bryan. As we walked in, I noticed June's eye, which was very red and oozing. I commented on it and she told me she'd gone down to the dispensary to get a treatment as it looked like pink eye, an infection usually caused by bacteria or a virus.

The following day, she called me in a panic. Her eye had swollen shut and turned black, and it was extremely painful, she said. I drove her back to the clinic and we both stood there in shock. At least fifty people were ahead of us, all with the same issue. This was a bad case of viral conjunctivitis.

There wasn't much the doctor could do. He told June and the others to apply cold compresses every thirty minutes and keep putting antibiotic drops in both eyes to ward off or treat any secondary infections.

By the next day, most of the expats, including all four in our family, had contracted it. It felt like we had sandpaper in our eyes, which at times would burn and other times were very itchy and constantly weeping.

Then someone pointed out that the medication the doctor had prescribed contained a high dose of mercury and was banned in Australia and other countries. We all immediately stopped using the drops, but now had nothing to treat our condition. It was a scary situation.

Luckily for us, Emperor Gold Mine intervened and got a shipment of acceptable medication flown over from Australia to treat its employees. It was still a good ten days of extreme discomfort, however, and left our eyes sensitive to light and dryness.

Eventually things started easing, and we all met at the golf club for a celebratory drink for having survived the worst of it, all of us wearing our sunglasses despite the fact that the sun had set. We sure did look a sorry bunch, but we understood how privileged we were compared to the rest of the country who did not have access to the safe medication.

I felt really helpless when the flu season hit a few months later, and every day the news report would give us the new number of deaths due to the flu. I was aware, of course, that people died from the illness, but first-world countries had access to the flu vaccine and offered it free of charge to people over 65. It was something we, frankly, took for granted, never for one second thinking of people from places like Africa, South America or the islands who didn't benefit from such treatment just because they couldn't afford it.

We'd been so arrogant in our comfy lives but living in Fiji opened my eyes to how the majority of the world lived, and how the financial state of a country decided the fate of its people. As I was listening to a new death toll, my mother-in-law in Australia called to tell us that she'd got her flu shot. I was so grateful for this, but at the same time a huge sadness and despair came over me for the elderly and sick Fijians who wouldn't be offered the vaccine.

I understood that this was how this world worked: the rich got richer while the poor kept on struggling. I couldn't change it, but I had very little tolerance for selfishness and stupidity, especially when it came from people who lived in a rich country and had never experienced any real trouble and knew nothing about what went on in other parts of the world, but still found things to complain about.

Bastille Day

The letter from the French Embassy invited my husband and I to attend the Bastille Day celebrations at the French ambassador's home in Suva, the capital.

Bastille Day, or *la fete Nationale*, as we French call it, is France's national day. It commemorates not only the storming of the Bastille on 14 July 1789, but also the day of the great federation on 14 July the following year, symbolising the fraternal union of all parties, and the freedom and equality of all French citizens.

We didn't really know what to expect but we were very excited. Not only were we going to a party at the ambassador's residence, but it was my and the kids' first trip down to Suva. Ivan had told us that it took a good four hours to get there, through the jungle and on rough roads.

We were excited to discover a new part of the island. We packed lots of toys, snacks and drinks to keep everyone happy for the drive, and headed off early on Friday morning. We turned right onto Kings Road towards RakiRaki, the first little farming town east of Vatukoula. The road suddenly opened up to the most breathtaking view, a panorama of the bluest ocean dotted with islands, the biggest ones being Wananu-i-ra ('Daydream of the West') and Wananu-i-cake ('Daydream of the East'). Then the road followed the curve of Viti Levu Bay before heading deep into the tropical rainforest.

From this point on, the road was unpaved. Ivan did his best to avoid the potholes, but we still ended up bouncing around, and quite soon we realised something was wrong with the car, which was tilting to one side. We had a flat.

'Don't worry,' said Ivan, confidently. 'This is to be expected. I'll get us up and going again in no time.'

We took advantage of the break to stretch our legs and enjoy the scenery. It was both peaceful and very noisy, with hundreds of birds chirping and the rustling of leaves in the trees – the total opposite of the west coast, where we lived, where it was so barren and dry. Here, we were surrounded by a dense, lush, tropical rainforest, the colours vibrant and saturated.

I watched Ivan change the tyre – something that was to come in useful a few months later, when I was heading into town for some groceries and I got a flat and ended up changing it myself.

We then all jumped back on board and continued our adventure. As we approached a village, we could hear a strange rhythmic sound. I asked Ivan if he knew what it was and he guessed it probably was some women making tapa, a traditional cloth made from the inner bark of the mulberry or fig tree. It's a lengthy process as it softens and expands through a series of soakings and beatings. The very intricate and beautiful patterns, Ivan explained, are obtained by applying paints or vegetable dyes of mostly brown, black or red. Sure enough, as we reached the village, we could see the ladies sitting together in a circle, chatting and laughing as they

Top: Bure are made of bamboo held together with magimagi, a fibrous product made from coconut husks, and with a roof thatched with coconut leaves.

Above: Friendly villagers waved as we drove by.

107

worked, beating the cloth with their wooden instruments.

As we passed more villages, I noticed once again the contrast with the western side of the island. Here the villages were built in a more traditional style, with the thatched huts called 'bure' more predominant, whereas on the other side, more modern materials such as bricks and corrugated iron were favoured.

Our slow progress was stopped a second time by a familiar tilt to the vehicle. Ivan and I looked at each other, knowing we were now in trouble, as we didn't have a second spare tyre.

'I'm going to have to hitchhike into the closest town from here. Hopefully, someone will be able to fix the tyre,' Ivan said.

Luckily, we didn't have to wait too long before a couple of men in a pickup truck came by and offered to take Ivan and the tyre with them. As I waved goodbye to my husband and stood alone with my two little kids on the side of the road in the middle of nowhere, I felt very small and lost.

Still, having Melina and Mansell with me gave me a purpose: to keep them calm, as I could see in their eyes the same uncertainty that I was feeling. So we sang songs, played 'I Spy', read a bit, and ate all the snacks, before finally we saw Ivan coming back, triumphantly holding up the repaired tyre. We all hugged and kissed him like we hadn't seen him in a month.

We arrived at the hotel in Suva with just enough time to shower, change and welcome the babysitter before jumping back into the car to go to the party. As we approached in our little old rattly car, we could see strings of limos, official cars with flags and chauffeurs, and fancy four-wheel-drives lining the streets. We drove quickly past, and finally parked (more like hid) a good kilometre down the street. Then we made our way on foot, back up to the house.

The property was magnificent, a beautiful colonial house surrounded by tropical vegetation. Thousands of lights were strung through the trees in the back yard, candles floated in the pool, and blue, white and red balloons gave it a romantic and yet vibrant and festive atmosphere. Waiters wove their way between joyful groups of people, offering champagne and canapés. We were told that most of the food had been flown in from France, and indeed the cheeses, cold cuts and pâtés were just like I remembered, divinely tasty.

We got chatting with a French couple who'd just sailed into Suva the day before. They told us how they'd left France five months earlier and were going around the world on their 36-foot Beneteau sailboat. They were amazed to hear that we were living in such a remote area, while we couldn't believe they were sailing, just the two of them, through the perilous oceans.

Our generous host appeared on stage and welcomed us all to his soirée. He introduced his guests of honour, dignitaries who'd flown in from the French-Polynesian island of Tahiti. Then the Fijian naval brass band struck up the French national anthem and we all joined in, singing our patriotic song while standing to attention and raising our glasses in unison to toast our great nation.

I was happy to notice that the terrible homesickness that had gripped me in the first few months away from France had now subsided and been replaced by a sense of pride at being an everyday ambassador of sorts for my country of origin. Our life was now more a fusion of old traditions and local ones.

*A guard outside Government House, the official residence of
the President of Fiji, in Suva.*

Cyclone Gavin

The cyclone season starts in November and runs until the end of April each year. A tropical depression was building over the southern Pacific Ocean, with the potential of becoming a tropical cyclone. We were at the beginning of March, so well into the cyclone season, but most times, these depressions ended up swerving and missing Fiji. They would usually dump a fair amount of rain but with no damage to any structures, so why would this time be any different?

These were our thoughts when Judy, June and I made plans to go down to Lautoka for a fun grocery-shopping and lunch outing. We were excited to shop at MH Morison's, the biggest supermarket in the region, because it stocked items we'd never see up in Tavua, where finding a box of chocolate cereal would be like striking gold. We each had a list of speciality items to pick up, knowing our families' favourite treats.

We arrived at around 11 am and went our separate ways up the aisles, gathering our treasures, noticing how busy the store seemed. Then we regrouped to plan the rest of our afternoon, which was to find a spot for a lazy lunch. We agreed on the tennis club, a nice casual setting, away from the hustle and bustle of the chaotic town.

It was surprisingly quiet there, and we were very happy to find a table in the shade. We all ordered the club sandwich and a huge glass of water. We were parched, and although a strong wind was blowing, it didn't help in the slightest to cool us down. It was very hot, with extreme levels of humidity.

We were enjoying our lunch, laughing over silly things, when suddenly the manager increased the volume on the radio station. It was that dreaded, doomsday-like music that announced the weather report. We all listened carefully, but not too worried, until we heard the words, 'It is now upgraded to a tropical cyclone and is heading straight for Viti Levu.' As if to emphasise the message, the strongest gust of wind yet blew through the place, knocking all the umbrellas down and tipping over glasses.

The manager came up to us and with a worried look said, 'I think this is going to be a bad one. Do you ladies live around here?'

'No,' said June. 'We're from Vatukoula.'

'Well, you should think about heading home soon,' he advised.

We quickly paid our bill and left, deciding to go back to the supermarket, this time for the essentials. The locals had been much smarter than us, however, and by the time we returned, the shelves were pretty empty. We still managed to grab some flour, rice, batteries, cans of soup, and lots and lots of bottles of water.

The happy-go-lucky atmosphere from our morning and lunch escapade was completely crushed, replaced by a sense of nervousness. June and I were eager to get home to our kids, while poor Judy was anxious to hear from her husband, who was away on the next island over, Vanua Levu. I invited her to come and stay with us, but she said she'd prefer to stay at her place with her old dog

Mitsy and wait by the phone in case Mick called.

We made it home in record time. The kids had heard about the cyclone but, like me, didn't really understand the implications, as we'd never experienced one.

Ivan phoned to warn me that he'd be late home that night. He had to ensure that all measures were in place for a worst-case scenario. I didn't ask what that meant.

By the next morning, the radio announcements were coming every thirty minutes. The kids were told to stay home from school. Ivan was taking paintings off the walls, strapping down the out-door furniture and putting masking tape diagonally across the windowpanes. He explained that if the windows shattered in the high winds that were expected, the masking tape would minimise the flying debris that could potentially be lethal.

'You should make us some meals, because once the electricity goes out, we'll be without a stove,' he suggested.

I quickly hopped into action, welcoming the distraction. I made a huge batch of chicken fried rice and a banana cake. I only realised once it was in the oven that I'd forgotten to put the eggs in – they were still standing on the counter. My mind definitely wasn't on cooking.

Ivan noticed my shaking hands and came over to hug me. 'It's going to be alright, love, don't worry,' he said. 'I lived through a big one last time I was here. The only thing I advise against is driving. I remember staying at the process plant late into the night, trying to keep it working, but unfortunately, the main motor finally shut down. We tried everything we could think of to get it going again but the freshwater pressure switch kept failing. It was only days later, when we could investigate what had caused the failure, that we found that it was a huge number of fish that had been sucked up from the raging river into the freshwater intake pipe, blocking and tripping the pump.'

'Poor fish!'

He nodded. 'I've never been so scared in my life on the drive home that night. The road was covered in debris, and I couldn't tell where it started or ended. I just knew I couldn't afford to run off the road – with winds howling at over a hundred kilometres per hour, it would've been way too dangerous to get out the car.'

'You're not helping my stress levels!' I told him.

He laughed and hugged me tighter. 'Sorry. But don't worry, these houses have been around for many decades. They're sturdy and will keep us safe.'

'What about Melita and her family?'

'The company has a few sturdy buildings at their disposal in case of emergencies. It's nothing the locals haven't seen before.'

'I did ask Melita if she wanted to bring the kids here, but she smiled and said for me not to worry, they'd be fine. But I feel better knowing they have somewhere to go in case of trouble,' I said.

At that moment, we saw a truck pull up outside our house. It was Emperor's maintenance crew, and they were unloading what looked like big sheets of wood.

'What are they doing?' I asked Ivan.

'They're going to hammer these over our windows on the outside. They'll serve as wooden shutters.'

Sure enough, they started nailing on the planks, gradually plunging the house into darkness as hardly any light could now enter, but better safe than sorry.

The kids came running in to ask what was happening, and I explained that we were going to have very strong winds, the same as we sometimes had in Carcassonne, and that the temporary wooden shutters would protect the windows. I could see Melina was thinking very hard about this, and she finally said, 'Yes, but Mum, we never had these weird wooden shutters on our windows in Carcassonne.'

She had a point.

▲ ▲ ▲

Tropical cyclones, or hurricanes, are the most damaging of all storms. They happen during the summer months when the ocean's surface temperature is 28 degrees Celsius or higher. The warm, moist air rises and forms a low-pressure cell, and as the temperature increases, the clouds start rotating around the low-pressure cell.

Cyclones are measured according to wind speed, with category 1 cyclones causing no damage to structures, and category 5 having extreme winds that pose a threat to houses and buildings.

It was now Friday morning, and Cyclone Gavin had been gathering strength for 24 hours, twisting and turning, and making it very difficult to determine if, where and when it would make landfall. It was determined to be a category 4 cyclone, and we were told to brace for major winds and potentially considerable damage.

I felt completely helpless and anxious, but I tried to keep a brave face on, as I could see that the kids were watching Ivan's and my every move.

An incredibly strong gust of wind came through and, just like that, three of our pawpaw trees came crashing down – I was looking through a slit in the wooden shuttering and saw them go over like skittles. 'It's okay,' Ivan said, as we looked at each other with panicked eyes. 'The pawpaw trees are always the first to go as their roots are so shallow.'

I suddenly had the urge to tell someone about our predicament – not that anyone could help, but it would comfort me to know that someone was aware of the danger we were facing and might be trying to reach us or at least get news of us in the days to come. I certainly couldn't call my parents, as it would be too stressful for them. I eventually settled on my eldest brother, Courtland.

He picked up on the second ring, happy to hear from me, but quickly realised that something was wrong by the sound of my voice. 'What's going on? Is everything okay?'

'So far we're doing okay but there's this big cyclone about to hit us and I just wanted you to know, as I'm not sure if the phones will go out, and if so, for how long.'

'Right!' is all I got out of him.

'I'll call you as soon as we're in the clear but if you don't hear from me, you can contact the French embassy in Suva.' One of the first things I'd done on arriving in Fiji was sign up with my embassy – in case of emergencies, they were the umbilical cord between their nationals and home.

'Okay,' Courtland said. 'Thanks for letting me know and try to stay safe.'

Shortly after the phonecall, the electricity went out. Things were really ramping up. The wind was howling, the rain fell in sheets, and the house was creaking and shaking.

Melina and Mansell had brought their toys into the dining room, and were playing under the sturdy dining table, while Ivan and I were playing cards on it. The table had lots of scratches and dents, and I smiled as I recalled the most recent addition. It was the letters M-E-L carved into the wood. When I'd first noticed them, I asked Melina what had happened, and she looked surprised and blurted out, 'It wasn't me, Mum. It was Mansell.'

'I doubt that very much, young lady, as your brother doesn't yet know how to spell your name. So try again,' I said, sternly.

'I really don't know why I did it. I wasn't thinking,' she said, as she burst into tears. 'I'm sorry!'

'That's okay, sweetie. I prefer you to admit your mistakes than to lie. Come here and give me a kiss.'

Ivan got up, bringing me out of my daydream, and headed towards the back of the house. I was surprised to see him opening a window there.

'Why are you doing that?' I asked.

'I just remembered that it's important to open a window on the opposite side from the wind direction,' he explained. 'A friend of mine learnt the hard way when their roof completely lifted off their house during a cyclone. It then came crashing back down, shattering all the ceilings on the upper level. It was caused by an imbalance in the pressure between the indoors and the outdoors. Keeping a window open prevents this from happening.'

▲ ▲ ▲

The day dragged on. The shadows dancing on the walls from the candlelight as well as the air moving through the curtains lent an eerie atmosphere to the already stressful situation. Our phone line was down so our only contact with the outside world was the faint voice of the radio host we could hear punctuated by crackling, static interference.

At 6 pm we had a dinner of cold fried rice and a slice of dry banana cake. Afterwards, for a bit of fun, we joined the kids under the table and pretended we were camping, Shadow, our dog, joined the party.

By 8:30 pm we were exhausted and decided we'd all sleep in one bed. Ivan's and my bed was only a double bed, but we managed to all squeeze in and spent a very long night, mostly lying awake, listening to the unfamiliar noises around us.

At 6 am, I awoke to the sound of dead silence.

Ivan, who'd woken up at around the same time, suddenly jumped out of bed and ran outside like a man possessed. 'What on earth are you doing?' I yelled, running after him.

'My avocados! I need to collect them before the local kids come and grab them all. I'm sure plenty fell during the strong winds.'

I stood in the front doorway, laughing, watching him scrambling around, picking up the fruit, and finally walking back with his arms full of avocados.

Ivan went outside again, and I went back to bed with the kids. About half an hour later, Ivan came in with a hot cup of instant coffee.

'How did you get hot water?' I asked, ecstatic at having my caffeine fix.

'I boiled some water on our barbecue!' he said proudly.

'McGyver has nothing on you! Thank you! I really need this today.'

Having had our morning pick-me-ups, we went outside and started assessing the damage. Most of the trees were at least partly if not completely down. And we could see cables that had been ripped off their poles dangling dangerously over the street.

'Well, at least the worst is over,' I said.

But Ivan shook his head. 'This isn't the end of it. We're probably in the eye of the cyclone, which is why it's so eerily quiet.'

Just as he said that, a strong gust of wind appeared out of nowhere.

'Here we go, round two,' Ivan said, and we all ran back inside.

It went on for another six long, boring hours.

Finally the rain abated and the wind died down. A huge sense of relief washed over me. I hadn't noticed how tense I'd been until the first ray of sun came shining through the clouds and I burst into tears. It was over and we were safe.

▲ ▲ ▲

A big tree had fallen on our neighbours' roof, but luckily no one was hurt. Melita's house had been destroyed, but her husband and friends were busy rebuilding it.

Within a couple of days, the maintenance crew had the phone lines back up and I was able to call my brother and tell him we were fine. He'd been tracking the cyclone and was relieved to hear from me.

The only expat in our immediate community who got injured was Judy. On Friday afternoon, during the worst of it, Mick had suddenly walked in the door. She couldn't believe he was standing in front of her, and as she ran towards him, she kicked her toe on the side of the kitchen counter, breaking it! (Mick later told us about his horrific drive home from the airport, and we were all grateful he'd made it back in one piece.)

At first glance the structure of the Tavua markets looked to be a complete mess of twisted metal and torn tarps, but later I compared the post-cyclone photo I took with one I'd taken a few days after arriving in Vatukoula and we actually couldn't see much difference. It gave Ivan and me a good laugh.

The electricity stayed out in Tavua for a week, and I'll never forget the stench of rotting meat that came out of the supermarket on the day it reopened. The meat had never looked very appetising, as it was hacked into big chunks, wrapped in plastic and thrown into the freezer; there was no telling what animal it was from, and I never bought any.

All that was left in the freezers, however, was the terrible smell. Out the front, the supermarket staff were selling meat curry for a dollar a plate.

Cyclone Gavin had been the strongest cyclone to hit the country since 1982–1983, with wind speeds over 185 kilometres per hour and gusts of 220. The damage done was estimated to be worth about US$23 million. Eighteen people lost their lives.

Melina's school collected items to donate to local villages that had been badly affected by the cyclone, and it was nice to see the human spirit of helping each other up again.

The flooding caused by Cyclone Gavin was severe, and a few days later when we went for a drive, we saw women with their shopping on their heads, wading through waist-deep waters. The long beautifully shaped leaves of the coconut palms were all dishevelled and broken.

Kids' stuff

Ivan and I had been trying for a baby since the day we'd got married, but every month we were left with a feeling of crushing disappointment when my period arrived.

I'd fallen pregnant really easily with Melina, but had had problems with subsequent pregnancies, miscarrying twice, so with the next pregnancy I was very closely monitored. My first ultrasound revealed I was carrying twins. The excitement was, alas, shortlived, as I suffered a major hemorrhage in my first trimester and lost one of the babies. The doctor ordered immediate bed rest and hormone injections every day for a month. I was overjoyed when my little baby boy was born, and I thank god every day for that miracle.

On a morning walk with my friend Kathy, I told her about Ivan's and my struggles to get pregnant. She'd just given birth to Andie, and suggested that I speak to her obstetrician, Dr Sandy.

Andie was Kathy's second child. Her first was a little curly-haired blonde 3-year-old cute-as-a-button monster called Isabel. Everyone's approach to raising their children is different, and Kathy and her husband Paul were both teachers who'd received an education in how to deal with the psyche of young children. In my eyes, that should've made them professionals, and knowledgeable about how to deal with tantrums, grumpiness or jealousy between siblings. Well, I'm sorry to say, but they sucked at it!

For example, when their darling angel daughter started having a tantrum, her mum, bless her heart, would spend a good ten minutes explaining to the hysterical child, in the calmest of voices, why it wasn't the time, right before lunch, to open the box of cookies. This one-sided conversation would continue while the child wailed on and on, and the whole neighbourhood would have to plug its ears.

I was torn between admiration for Kathy's stamina and annoyance at the stupidity of the whole situation. I couldn't see anything wrong with the way I did things: I would explain once, or maybe twice, in case there was a language or understanding problem, and then it would be time-out in the bedroom until the child felt like communicating with me in a sensible manner.

Things had gotten exponentially worse with Isabel since the arrival of Andie, her new baby brother.

Kathy and the kids came over for a visit one day, while my two were at school. All was well while little Andie was sleeping. Isabel was being surprisingly cute and playing with some toys her mum had brought with her. The minute little Andie started stirring, however, needing his mother's attention, things went downhill fast.

As Kathy started breastfeeding the baby, Isabel told her mother she needed to pee. I offered to take her to the toilet, but I got a thunderous look from the monster, as if to say, 'I wasn't talking to you!'

Kathy said, 'Let me just get Andie positioned, then I'll take you.'

Isabel's response to that was to pull up her dress and pee through her knickers, right there, on my dining-room floor.

I couldn't believe my eyes. Kathy was terribly embarrassed and offered to clean up the mess while looking after the baby and holding a conference with Isabel on how she was sorry she'd failed her in her moment of need. Oh boy!

I ran off to get the mop – I had to get out of there, breathe deeply and do a quick meditation session before I could trust myself not to lose it with the mum or the child.

A few days later, I was at home getting lunch ready when the phone rang. It was Kathy. 'Hi Fiona,' she said. 'I wanted to let you know that we've just been to the markets, and Isabel fell in love with these two little chicks. I thought it would be a good idea to get them for her to look after. I have Andie and she has her chicks. What do you think?'

'Well, yes, I guess,' I said, doubtfully. I wasn't really feeling it but why not?

'You should see her with them, she's so caring and loving,' Kathy continued. 'She's busy giving one a big hug ...' At that moment, Kathy's voice became a shriek. 'Oh no, Isabel! No, no! Don't do that, sweetie, you might hurt him. Oh no!'

'Kathy, are you okay? What's happened?'

Kathy was now crying. 'She literally hugged that poor chick to death. He's dead! She strangled it!' she sobbed. 'That poor little chick would still be alive if we hadn't bought him. You must help me!'

'Me? How? What can I do?'

'You must rescue the second one. Please take him or she'll kill it too.'

'Oh, I don't think I want to, I'm not really—' I began, but she'd already hung up.

Five minutes later she was on my doorstep, handing me a box with the little guy and his food. 'Thank you, Fiona! You're a life saver – literally!' she said, and off she went.

I stood there, trying to understand what had just happened.

I eventually headed back into the kitchen and took the little yellow bird out of its box. It jumped onto my slipper and never stopped chirping, even when I walked around the house.

Ivan's look when he came home for lunch was priceless – a mixture of astonishment and concern (probably for the state of my mental health). After I explained the crazy morning's events, he proceeded to give me a lesson on how to be a good mother hen. 'He's saying, "Pick me up!" Birds like to be on people's shoulders.'

'Aren't you getting confused with parrots? I've seen cartoons with pirates and parrots, but I'm not sure it applies to chickens.'

Ivan picked up the little bird and positioned it on his shoulder. 'See how happy he is up here?'

At that precise moment, the little bird let go all down Ivan's shirt. As he tried to hand the chick to me and get his shirt off over his head without ending up with chicken poop on his face, I laughed until I cried.

That afternoon, Kathy called to ask how things were going. I said that the chick was chirping loudly and I didn't know how to make him stop, and she came up with the brilliant idea of going

back to the markets the following morning to get another chick –
it was obvious to her that this one was missing its dead mate.

This time I did put my foot down, however. I decided I would
ask Melita if she thought the village would like a new member, and
Melita was only too happy to take the chick.

So the little bird was sorted out, but that wasn't the last run-in
we had with the monster child.

On one of our weekends in Nadi, who should we bump into
at the entrance of a casual family restaurant but Kathy and her
family. Ivan saw them first and invited them to share a table with
us before I could intervene. Luckily, we were offered a table in a
small room at the back of the restaurant, because the problems
started as soon as we sat down.

Within minutes, the child had pulled the curtains off their rod,
and then her shoe went flying across the table, smacking Ivan in
the nose before landing in his plate. I could see by Ivan's face that
he was deeply regretting his offer to share a table, but I was rather
enjoying watching him struggle – I'd told him how atrocious this
kid was, but he'd never witnessed it, so he continually played it
down. Not this time.

When Isabel proceeded to screech, demanding her shoe back,
he told her to come over and get it. Reluctantly, she did, but as she
was leaving, she gave him the evil eye and muttered, 'I don't like
you.'

'Same here, young lady,' Ivan told her.

Then she marched over to Mansell, pulled him towards her,
and bit him hard in the neck. The poor little boy screamed and
shoved her away, and she fell onto her backside and started crying.

We were all up by this stage, Ivan and I comforting Mansell, who had a huge bite mark on his neck, while Isabel's parents were hugging her, promising to get her an ice cream to forget about what the naughty boy had done to her.

Then, astonishingly, Paul turned to Mansell and said, 'Shame on you, young man. This is no way to treat a younger friend. If you want to pick on someone, find someone your own age.'

It was an absolute miracle that Ivan didn't have it out with Paul. While he was still reeling in shock at Paul's comment, I was able to usher him and the kids towards the car, wave goodbye and make a quick getaway.

After that, I only ever saw Kathy when Ivan, Melina and Mansell weren't present.

▲ ▲ ▲

Based on the Gold Coast, an hour south of Brisbane in Australia, Kathy's doctor, Dr Sandy, was the head of a fertility clinic there. During a phonecall with him the next evening, his advice was that the first thing to do was to have Ivan's sperm count checked. The only laboratory that could do the necessary measurement was in Lautoka, so we stayed overnight in a hotel there so that Ivan could deliver his sperm within the thirty-minute survival period. The results were disappointing: the count was extremely low, with only 2 000 little swimmers.

When we called to tell Dr Sandy the results, to our surprise, he burst out laughing. 'That's impossible,' he said. 'I don't think they know what they're doing over there.'

It turned out that a low sperm count was considered fifteen million or fewer, and the fact that Ivan's count was only 2 000 meant that the problem was with the lab's calculations, not with his swimmers.

'Is there any way you could come over to my clinic for a recount?' Dr Sandy asked.

We arranged it immediately, leaving the children with Mick and Judy for the four days we'd be away. It was our first time off the island in over six months, so when we arrived at our hotel in Surfers Paradise on the Gold Coast, we quickly dumped our suitcases in our room and headed out to explore our surroundings and find a place for dinner. We were overwhelmed by all the possibilities – did we want Italian, French, Chinese, Thai ...?

The next day we arrived a good twenty minutes ahead of our scheduled appointment. It was great to meet Dr Sandy in person, and we both found him approachable and easy to talk to. He welcomed our questions and spent a lot of time explaining the pros and cons of IVF treatment. He explained that there were no guarantees, that it was expensive, and that it would be a tough process for me to go through, as my body would be pumped full of hormones and the side effects would include mood swings, headaches, fatigue, abdominal pain, breast tenderness and more.

Ivan handed over his sperm sample before we headed to a coffee shop and sat down to talk it over. We both felt the odds were really low for the price tag, and Ivan was especially concerned about not putting my health at risk. We already had a beautiful family, he said, and he was quite happy to let it be.

Baby-making

A week after our Australia trip, Ivan's father, Brian, came to visit us in Fiji. I was quite apprehensive at first about having him stay, as I didn't know him very well. I'd only met him once before, when he'd come to France for our wedding. All I knew was that he'd recently separated from his wife, and that that had caused some friction between Ivan and him. Ivan was very close to his mum and didn't understand the reason for his father's decision.

Brian turned out to be quite charming and easy to talk to. He was happy to sit and play with the children or join me on my grocery-shopping outings. He liked talking about his native South Africa, where the family had lived in Pietermaritzburg and he'd practised as a dental prosthetist for twenty years before deciding to move to Australia. Like many others in his situation, he'd found it heartbreaking to leave his life and livelihood behind but had felt it was the only way to ensure the best future for his three children.

Brian stayed for ten days, and I really enjoyed his company and having someone to talk to while the kids and Ivan were out during the day. We went to the markets, Ivan took him for a tour of the mine, and he had a go at golf.

On his last weekend, we went to Nadi, where we took him to

our favourite restaurant, Chefs. The meal didn't sit well on my stomach, and on the ride home, I had to ask Ivan to stop the car as I was feeling really nauseous.

As we passed the pharmacy, I suddenly told Ivan to pull over, and I rushed in to pick up a pregnancy test. We'd been down this route before, and we knew better than to get excited, but nothing ventured, nothing gained.

At home, a big yellow envelope was waiting for us in the mailbox – it turned out to be the report from Dr Sandy about Ivan's sperm count, which was good. His sperm were not, however, energetic swimmers, and died off rapidly, making it, in the doctor's professional opinion, very unlikely that we could ever conceive naturally. We felt crushed.

I still felt a bit sick, so I decided to do the pregnancy test anyway, in spite of the fact that it seemed almost certain it would be negative.

But it wasn't.

I was pregnant!

▲ ▲ ▲

'That's wonderful news!' said my Fijian friend Susana. 'And I know the perfect doctor for you. He's probably brought half of Fiji's population into the world. He was my doctor for my four children. They made him come out of retirement because there's no one more knowledgeable or experienced. He's literally irreplaceable!'

'He sounds very old,' I said, doubtfully. 'Are you sure he's still up to it?'

'He's probably in his 60s but he's very hale and hearty – he's actually a marathon runner. I know him very well. Let me call and set up a meeting for you.'

As the days went by, the morning sickness became so bad that it lasted all day. I didn't mind – I was pregnant, and that was all that mattered.

The day of the appointment with Dr Batta finally arrived, and I did the seventy-kilometre drive down to the hospital in Lautoka, where he had his practice, on my own. I ended up stuck behind an open-backed truck on which a couple of men were dissecting a pig, which didn't help with my nausea at all. I couldn't overtake, and neither could I close my eyes, obviously, as I was driving. It felt like I was trapped in a horror movie with no escape.

When I spotted a sign for an upcoming side road, I gratefully turned onto it, stopped the car, leapt out and threw up right there on the side of the dusty road. I sat there for a while, waiting for the shakes to subside and feeling quite sorry for myself.

I was still sweating profusely when I got to the hospital. The grandfatherly Dr Batta was very gentle and solicitous. 'Good morning, my dear. My, you look quite flushed,' he said, concerned. 'Please come in and take a seat. Let me get you a glass of water.'

We went over my medical history and he was, of course, very interested in my previous pregnancies and deliveries – both Caesarean sections, thanks to my very narrow pelvis. Dr Batta calculated the due date to be around the third week in January. Then it was time for the physical exam.

'We don't have ultrasound machines here, so all I can do is listen to the heartbeat and examine you,' Dr Batta explained apologetically. 'Go into the booth in the corridor, remove your clothes and put on the gown.'

I did as I was instructed, and after a few minutes, a nurse called me into a tiny room, just big enough for a bed. It had no door for privacy, just a curtain precariously held up by two pegs. I tried distracting myself by focusing on the fan oscillating above my head. It was absolutely filthy and had obviously never been cleaned. That got me thinking about the instruments and other rooms in this hospital – again, not where my mind should have been going.

The examination over, Dr Batta was happy to report that all looked well, and that the heartbeat was strong and healthy. He came back a few minutes later with a prescription. 'Something to ease the morning sickness. I'll see you again in a couple of months. In the meantime, rest as much as possible. And don't worry – everything will be okay.'

I thanked the kindly doctor, but I knew in my heart that if there was one thing I wasn't about to do, it was to take any medication whatsoever for my nausea. After our experience with the eye drops, I didn't trust Fiji's medicine. I'd heard ginger was good for treating nausea, and there was plenty of that around, so I was good.

▲ ▲ ▲

On my next visit, my friendly doctor wasn't looking so good, with a grey pallor to his complexion and his usually smiley face scrunched up as if in pain. 'Is everything alright?' I asked, as I lay on the examination bed.

'All is well,' he said, reassuringly. 'You're doing just fine.'

'I was actually asking about you – you don't look happy today?'

'I have a terrible headache,' he admitted.

'Well, Doctor, you should go home and rest. That's what you always tell me to do.'

'You're right. I think I'm going to do that. I'm running in the Suva marathon the day after tomorrow.' Billed as the South Pacific's greatest road race, it covered 42,2 kilometres. 'I'm old now so it will be a very slow run.'

'That's quite the endeavour!' I said. 'I'll be thinking of you.'

'Thank you, my dear. I'll tell you all about it next month when I see you.'

But I never got to see dear Dr Batta again. He collapsed and died of a brain aneurism while running the marathon. The news made the front page of the *Fiji Times*, and his funeral was attended by thousands of people who wanted to pay their respects to the doctor who'd helped so many women.

I was devastated by the news, of course, and after the shock had passed came the realisation that I was now over four months pregnant and without a doctor.

Bruno, another expat from the mine, had just welcomed a baby boy. His wife, Kellesi, a local, told me she'd been quite happy with the service at the Tavua hospital, but I just couldn't wrap my head around how primitive it was. She'd had to take her own sheets and insect repellent as the windows had no flyscreens.

While these were only minor details, they did make me wonder about their operating gear, and what about incubators? And I'd be giving birth right in the middle of cyclone season – if another Cyclone Gavin came along right when I was due to deliver, I can only imagine what kind of chaos and stress there would be.

Ivan and I had contacted Dr Sandy to find out what the price of a delivery by C-section would be in Australia – we had no medical insurance in that country, so if we decided to go there, it would be entirely at our own expense. He sent us the detailed cost of the average procedure. Ivan did the maths and came up with a total cost of Aus$5 000. We felt this was unaffordable.

'We need to find a doctor we trust on this island,' said Ivan, so I called the French Embassy in Suva for some recommendations. They told me about Dr VolaVola, a British-trained obstetrician practising at the Suva Hospital, 200 kilometres from our home.

I made an appointment and headed down to Suva the following week.

Dr VolaVola was incredibly patient with me, as I grilled him with my million questions. Yes, the hospital had generators in case of electricity failures. They were in perfect working order and were regularly tested. The hospital had three incubators, none in working order, but they were expecting new ones before my due date.

I left feeling marginally better but we still were doubtful about chancing the delivery in Fiji. Finally, a conversation with my brother, Courtland, decided things for us. 'Is a healthy baby not worth $5 000?' he asked.

He was right: we'd just been too caught up in the details to step back and see the bigger picture.

We rang Dr Sandy and asked him to keep a date open in January for the delivery. At the same time we made an appointment for our one and only ultrasound at his clinic in Brisbane, in September, in five weeks' time. We were relieved and, finally, very excited.

All creatures great and small

In August, Ivan was to attend a conference in Singapore for a week, and we decided to make it a family vacation. From there we would go to Brisbane to have our much-anticipated ultrasound.

Flying with Air Pacific was quite an adventure on its own. Fijians always packed lots of boxes to take with them, either to family in Australia or for bringing supplies back into Fiji, so a long wait at customs was the norm. It always amazed me to see all these rickety cardboard boxes going round on the conveyor belt – they didn't look very secure and yet they always seemed to make it without completely disintegrating and spilling out their precious contents.

Then, when we were in the air, a very intoxicated Fijian started getting quite aggressive, and while the flight attendants politely tried to get him under control, it became clear that he wasn't going to cooperate. As they were frantically trying to locate the pair of handcuffs they presumably had on board, one of his mates who'd had enough of his drunken behaviour simply decked him twice, knocking him out for the remainder of the flight. I was quite horrified, but I have to admit that it did sort out the commotion.

Singapore was very regimented but also impeccably clean. Famous for its numerous rules and regulations, you could get fined for any number of banned things, including chewing gum, singing obscene lyrics in public, annoying anyone with a musical instrument, forgetting to flush the toilet, and spitting. I noticed many tourist T-shirts making fun of this, with slogans such as 'Singapore is a fine city' or 'I went to Singapore and didn't get fined!'

I was very happy to find western shops, so while Ivan was busy at his conference, the kids and I hit the stores armed with my lengthy list – something that worried Ivan a bit, as Singapore isn't known to be the cheapest place on earth! We also enjoyed doing some sightseeing and travelling on Singapore's amazing transit system.

I was intrigued by the sign telling people it was forbidden to transport durian, a fruit, on the subway – until I got a whiff of it in a local market. It smells like a mixture of rotten meat, turpentine and used gym socks. The locals told me it tasted better than it smelled but I was happy to just take their word for it.

When Ivan was done with work, we took the kids to the Singapore Zoo. I'm not a zoo fan, but this one was extremely spacious, with every habitat replicating what the animal would need in the wild. Mansell loved the monkeys and Melina the dolphins and penguins. The only part I didn't enjoy was when a handler put a massive boa constrictor on Ivan's shoulders; I've never been a fan of reptiles.

We were at the local airport, waiting to check in for our flight to Brisbane, when we got the news that Lady Diana Spencer had been killed in a car accident in a tunnel in Paris. This hit home for two reasons, the first being that the accident had happened in Paris, and we'd driven countless times through that very tunnel. Also, and the thing that I think shocked the world, was how such a mundane yet tragic accident could happen to such an iconic person.

▲ ▲ ▲

At the doctors' rooms, after the routine check-up, we headed over to the ultrasound machine. This would be our first time seeing our little baby, and we felt very emotional and apprehensive. But Dr Sandy quickly put us at ease – everything was looking normal, and the baby was a good size and a good weight, with all its toes and fingers, and a strong heartbeat. We breathed a sigh of relief.

'Are you interested in knowing what you're having?' Dr Sandy asked.

'Yes, please!' we said in unison. We were struggling to decide on a name, as Ivan loved the exoticness of the French ones and I preferred English ones. Knowing would cut our debates by half.

'It's a little girl.'

Ivan took my hand kissed it. 'Perfect,' he said.

▲ ▲ ▲

With light hearts, we headed to the amusement park. Ivan and I got caught up in the excitement with the kids – it was so much fun to feel like a child again. We went from one attraction to the other, all having an amazing time. Melina was thrilled to see Scooby-Doo, the Great Dane from the cartoon series of the same name, and with a squeal of joy ran up to give him a big hug.

Mansell had only one wish, and that was to see the Batmobile – and suddenly, there it was, just like in his dreams, except better, as Batman himself was standing next to it with his arms crossed, looking very serious indeed. Batman was Mansell's absolute favourite superhero. Desperate to meet his hero but suddenly overcome with shyness, Mansell finally grabbed Ivan's hand. 'Come with me, Dad,' he said.

They approached gingerly and Batman suddenly made eye contact with him. 'What's your name, son?' the superhero asked in his incredibly deep and powerful voice.

'Mansell,' squeaked Mansell, hiding behind Ivan's legs.

'Pleased to meet you!' Batman boomed. 'Come shake my hand!'

Mansell went home that day with a Batman T-shirt complete with a cape, and he wore it nonstop for a whole year. I would have to nag him to take it off to be washed, and he'd always secretly ask Melita to do a rush job, as he needed it back quickly. She always graciously agreed. Those two were as thick as thieves.

▲ ▲ ▲

Mansell (with Ivan) got to shake Batman's hand and never stopped
talking about it for the rest of the day. 'Batman shook my hand!'
he kept saying, waving the hand at us.

Back in Fiji, one beautiful Thursday in October, Jackie invited ten of us women out for a boat ride. She and her husband Phil were one of the few expat couples who owned a boat, and they were extremely gracious in often asking others to join them on outings.

It was a glorious day, sunny, with a soft breeze blowing. We heaved all our equipment on board, then ourselves; I was now six months pregnant and finding it more challenging to move around.

We set off on the beautiful ocean. It was exhilarating, bouncing on the waves, wind in the hair, sun on our faces.

We'd been going for a good twenty minutes when Jackie reduced the speed and told us we were now in an area where she usually encountered dolphins. She tapped on the side of the boat, something she found, she said, sometimes attract them. We waited impatiently, eyes peeled on the water around us. Suddenly, one jumped out of the ocean, right at our side. We all clapped and cheered; we could hardly believe our eyes.

Soon there were more dolphins, looking at us with their beautiful smiley faces. One woman jumped overboard to join them, then another, then another, until only Jackie, the captain, and I were left on board. I so wanted to get into the water, but the boat didn't have a ladder and I knew that I would battle to get back in. Still, I was happy just to photograph the encounter, as the dolphins jumped around the swimmers as if playing tag.

'Shouldn't we be looking out for sharks?' I asked Jackie, suddenly remembering this was the Pacific Ocean, not the Mediterranean, where, although sharks are present, sightings are rare and attacks on swimmers even rarer.

'No, they're fine,' Jackie assured me. 'Sharks are scared of dolphins, and you can see the women are surrounded by dolphins.'

There were about twenty of these amazing marine mammals now, swimming around. As we were speaking, we watched a dolphin leap out of the water and perform an astonishing twist in the air, before splashing back down.

'That was just incredible!' I said.

'Yes, these are called spinner dolphins. They're very social and love to put on a show. That's one of their party tricks, spinning along their longitudinal axis while leaping through the air. I once saw one spin four times before diving back into the water.'

For me, the 'show' the dolphins were putting on was even more amazing because no one was making them jump for spectators – they were just being natural wild dolphins. I hugged Jackie and thanked her for sharing this beautiful experience with us.

One by one, we helped the women get back on board. They all felt the same gratitude for having had the opportunity to share such a special encounter.

As Jackie started the boat and we headed off slowly, the dolphins kept pace with us, as if they were egging us on for a race. Jackie pushed the throttle forward, and as we gained speed, so did they, in a frenzy of jumps and spins. It was sheer delight to watch them. We laughed and cheered them on until they finally turned and left us.

Jackie found us a sandbank to anchor and enjoy some lunch. It was surreal, standing on the pristine, white, sandy patch of land in the ocean. The water around us was crystal clear, and we could see colourful fish swimming just a few metres from us.

It was a day that will live on in my memory as one of the best of my life.

Dogs and horses

For some unknown reason, one of the surprising characteristics of a majority of the dogs in Fiji is that they have short legs. Shadow, our dog, who otherwise looked like a Doberman, was no exception. She was a good watchdog but the kids didn't like playing with her, as she was very strong and would always end up knocking them over.

One morning I received a frantic call from Melina's teacher. It appeared Shadow had escaped and followed Melina to school. By the time I got there, I found all the kids either standing on their chairs or sitting on their tables, trying to escape Shadow, who thought it was a great game. She was barking and jumping and running around the classroom. It was complete chaos.

Apologising profusely, I quickly caught Shadow and marched her home. As I left, I looked back and saw Melina giving me the death stare. But Shadow seemed pretty happy with her morning's antics and didn't understand why I was so upset with her.

We knew that, aged about six months, Shadow would soon go into heat, and obviously we wanted to get her spayed, but the last time the vets had come to town she'd been too young. So now we had to endure her heat cycle, and for the last three days and nights, we'd been battling a constant string of males coming by the house to try their luck with Miss Shadow. As the houses were slightly raised off the ground to maximise airflow, it enabled her suitors to get right under her room and howl constantly. And she was just as frantic to meet them.

We had to let her out occasionally to do her business, and we restricted her to the back deck. Still, although we had barricades up at the gate and the deck was a few metres above ground, we got caught out by an exceptionally athletic boy, and before we knew it, the deed was done.

Within a month or so it became evident that Shadow was pregnant, and she was slowing down a little, just as I was. But dogs carry for only about two months. 'Lucky you,' I told her. 'You'll be done soon. I still have three months to go.'

One night, Ivan and I decided to have a date night at the bowling club. It was just across the street from our home, so he'd go straight there from work, and I'd join him as soon as Melita had arrived to mind the children. But late that afternoon, I couldn't find Shadow. She'd taken to resting on the front doorstep, but she wasn't there, and although I kept calling her, she just didn't show up.

Suddenly, I heard a faint noise coming from the laundry room. Peering in, I saw Shadow lying on a towel and it was immediately obvious that she was in labour.

I stayed with her for the next few hours, comforting her. Soon she'd pushed out three little puppies, but then she started yelping and looking very uncomfortable. She was obviously struggling to push the next one out, so I helped her, gently pulling as she pushed. When the puppy was finally born, she quickly got to work cleaning it, as she'd done with the others. It was my first time witnessing a dog giving birth, and I was very impressed by how she instinctively knew what to do.

Once all eight pups had been born and thoroughly cleaned by their mama, Shadow gently guided them to feed. I left her to enjoy a much-needed rest.

When Melita arrived at 7 pm, I said goodnight to the little ones and headed up the garden path towards the street. Suddenly, an animal came flying at me, its eyes crazed, biting me in the stomach and on the arms. It took me a few moments to realise it was Shadow.

'Melita! Help!' I screamed, trying to protect my baby and at the same time find something to defend myself with. I managed to get hold of a stick and hit out at Shadow, all the while retreating back towards the house.

Melita came running out, screaming at Shadow, and dragged me back inside. I was bleeding, crying and shaking all over. My stomach showed teeth marks and was already starting to bruise, and I was so scared that something had happened to the baby.

We were too afraid to go outside again, so Melita phoned the neighbours, who got hold of Ivan and asked him to come home.

My husband was obviously shocked to see the state I was in. Arming himself with a stick, he went outside to find Shadow and try to work out what had happened. But by then, she was back to normal, calm and busy feeding her babies.

We decided it must have been an overprotective instinct that took hold after she'd given birth. I was cautious around her for a few days after the unexpected attack but soon realised that I had nothing more to fear. Although my stomach stayed black and blue

Mansell and Shadow.

for many days, my little baby had been well protected and didn't suffer from the attack.

The puppies were very cute and attracted a lot of attention. Mansell was in love with one of the boys, who had a distinctive mark on his forehead. It was like the Nike sign, so that became his name.

A few weeks later, as Ivan was leaving for work, he noticed Shadow acting very strangely, so he went to investigate. Someone had come during the night and stolen all the puppies. The poor mum was distraught and frantically looking for her babies. We were all so upset.

Melita asked people in the village about them, but they were never found.

Mansell took it the hardest. He'd loved his little Nike and remained inconsolable for many days.

▲ ▲ ▲

The Melbourne Cup is a horse race held annually on the first Tuesday of November in Melbourne, Australia. It's as famous there as the Epsom Derby is in England or the Kentucky Derby in the USA.

The Sheraton Fiji down in Nadi put on a luncheon to celebrate this event. A few of us, including Judy, Jackie, June, Anita and I, decided to attend. As is tradition for these events, most women wear a hat, and the Sheraton put on a competition for the best hat. The rules were that it had to be handmade, big and eccentric.

We knew Jackie would participate, as she's a very talented artist with an amazing imagination, and we waited in anticipation to see what she'd created. She didn't disappoint, turning up wearing a huge saucer with a cup full of what looked like foamy milk with a spoon in it. She won first prize, of course – a weekend for two at the resort hosting this event.

The success of the hat competition gave Jackie the idea to hold a country-and-western night at our local golf club. People were to dress up in their best country-and-western look, and Raj would provide his famous stuffed rotis for the hungry crowd.

It was a great turnout. Everyone came dressed in plaid shirts, jeans, cowboy boots and hats, and some of us even put on pretty good Texan accents.

Not only that, but ten of us women got to perform our line-dancing routines. Before coming to Fiji, Judy had lived in Tamworth, a mining town known to be the country-music capital of Australia. And where there's country music, there's line dancing. Judy had taken lessons and was eager to show us a few routines.

I'd always loved dancing, so I was the first to put my hand up. Ten of us met every Tuesday morning at Judy's house to kick our heels up to the sounds of 'Boot Scootin' Boogie' or 'Achy Breaky Heart'. It took a lot of practice, and there was a lot of knocking into each other, flailing arms and tripping before we managed to dance in unison, but eventually we got pretty good.

Our routine was a great hit, but by that time I was seven months pregnant, and after our half-hour show, I was exhausted. I could feel my baby giving me some good kicks in the ribs, as if to say, 'Settle down, Mother, it's getting a little too bouncy in here!'

▲ ▲ ▲

Jackie and Phil get into the spirit of things as the top and tail of a horse at the country-and-western party at the golf club.

One morning, after school dropoff, I was busy tidying the house when I heard a strange noise at the front door. I opened it to see ... a horse. Then a little wrinkled face popped out from behind the animal, holding up a bag. 'Would you like to buy some prawns?'

'I won't buy the prawns, but I will buy your horse,' I said.

The toothless old man looked at me, completely puzzled. What he couldn't know was that I'd loved horses since I was a little girl and had always dreamt of one day owning my own horse. Now a horse was right here, on my doorstep. How could this not be a sign?

'But madam, how will I get home? He is my means of transportation,' the old man explained.

'A taxi?' I suggested, hopefully, on the unlikely off-chance that he'd agree.

'Is Bosso here?' he asked.

And there it was: he was dismissing me as merely the wife, whose words held no value. He wanted to talk to the man in charge.

I recalled some months before, being at the bank and trying to get Ivan's and my chequebook – both our names were on the account – and the bank manager insisted on seeing my husband so that he could sign for it. It made me realise that the lack of respect for women – of all nationalities – in Fiji was really bothering me. Even when somebody came to our door to sell us mangoes or some other product, as now, they would always ask for 'the boss'. It drove me crazy.

Ivan tried to make me feel better by joking about it, saying, 'We both know who the real boss is in this house,' but that didn't help. 'You tell them that!' I would say, huffing and puffing.

Anyway, in this instance, with the old man, I let it go because, after all, I was sounding like a crazy woman – he was selling prawns and I wanted to buy his horse. 'If you want to wait, my husband will be home for lunch in a few minutes,' I told him.

So he tied his horse to a tree and settled down for a nap.

Shortly after 12, Ivan pulled up in front of the house. His expression when he saw the horse and the sleeping old man was priceless – half intrigued, half amused. I explained to him about my deep desire to own a horse, and he went outside to negotiate.

A few minutes later he was back, holding a bag of prawns. 'He really needs his horse – but look, his prawns look delicious!' he said.

I gave Ivan a grumpy look, but I had to admit that it probably wasn't the best time to get a horse. I was weeks away from having our baby, and we definitely had more pressing matters to deal with.

Fun with food

I wasn't a keen cook, and I never had to cook when I worked at the hotel – we used to just get food delivered from our closest restaurants. So my dishes were often the result of trial and error.

To make things worse, because I'm French, people seemed to automatically expect a Michelin-star meal when they came over. For this, I had a plan. I'd perfected my boeuf bourguignon and a tarte tatin. So guests were usually only invited for dinner once, as that was my only menu, or they'd have to be prepared to eat the same thing again and again.

Of course, it was harder to trick Ivan, as he lived with me, and it didn't help that he was a foodie. One day he came home from the shops with a corned beef. I'd never eaten one, let alone cooked one – and then he said the words no wife ever wants to hear: 'My mum makes the best corned beef and white sauce ever!'

One day I bumped into Ethan at the markets, and invited him to join us for dinner the following Saturday night. I felt sorry for the poor fellow: Ivan had told me that his wife had run off with another expat a few years back, and that he'd been on his own ever since.

We already had some steaks, so, on the Friday before the

dinner, I headed into Tavua to see what I could find for starters, veggies and a dessert. I was delighted to find some cabbages in the supermarket, which weren't our favourite vegetable, but it was the first time I'd ever seen a cabbage in Fiji. I grabbed one quickly, and almost put it back just as quickly when the cashier told me the price – twenty dollars! That was ten times the price I was used to paying for a cabbage back in France!

Next, I headed over to the markets, where I picked up some avocados. I always felt sad having to buy them, as our beautiful avocado tree had been chopped down by mistake. Ivan had told the maintenance crew about a tree branch hitting our power line and asked if they could remove it. They did a very thorough job, removing not only the branch but the whole tree. The problem was it was the whole wrong tree – the avocado tree.

When Ivan got home from work, he was understandably very upset that his precious little tree was gone. And it didn't help that still there, standing proud and creaking above our heads, was the offending branch, still hitting the power line, as if mocking him.

I came home with my groceries, a menu taking shape in my head. For a starter we'd have a salad of olives, avocado, lettuce and tomato; for mains we'd have the steaks, potatoes and cabbage; and I'd make a chocolate cake for dessert.

On the Saturday morning, I got right into making the cake. For me, dessert is the most important part of a dinner, and I feel that if the dessert is done well, the dinner will be a success.

The kids were playing in the bath, and I'd just taken the cake out of the oven when they called me to help them wash their hair. I was gone from the kitchen for no longer than fifteen minutes but when I returned, I realised I'd made a rookie mistake. I'd left the cake to cool on the counter, and it was covered in thousands of sugar ants – it actually looked alive, as if it was moving.

I was so mad at myself. I knew that the only way to safely leave a cake to cool here was to put some water in the bottom of the sink with a glass in the middle, basically creating a moat, and then balance the cake on top of that.

I had throw the cake away, and I had no time to make another one. I rummaged through the freezer and found some ice cream. That would have to do.

Ivan got home from work just before Ethan was due to arrive.

'What's that weird smell?' he asked as he came through the door.

'I found a cabbage at the store. Isn't that nice, for a change?' I said, proudly.

'I didn't think we liked cabbage,' Ivan said uncertainly.

'Yes, but Ethan is English and the English love cabbage,' I said, confidently.

'Where did you hear that?' he asked, looking really puzzled.

Just then we heard a knock at the door, so I was spared answering as I went to open it.

We sat out in the back garden with our guest, Ivan barbecuing our steaks, while we chatted and watched the sun set, sipping on a few beers.

'Ethan, I forgot to ask if you were allergic to anything,' I said, more or less just making conversation.

'Nope,' he said, 'but I do hate olives and avocado.'

I turned to Ivan with a look of quiet panic: olives and avocado were the main ingredients in my starter.

Ivan shrugged and smiled, then said, 'Love, maybe we need a few slices of bread with some butter on the table.' Nothing fazes my husband.

We ate our salad quickly, while I tried not to feel too bad about Ethan having to pick out half the ingredients.

I cleared the table, taking the dishes to the kitchen, where Ivan joined me. 'Hopefully your theory about the English loving cabbage is right,' he whispered, grinning.

'Shut up,' I said. I was starting to feel a little out of sorts.

Ivan brought the steaks to the table while I served the cabbage and the potatoes. I passed the plate to Ethan, who, to my shock, burst into tears.

'It's okay, mate, you don't have to eat it,' Ivan said. 'I told Fiona that no one likes that stuff.'

'It's not that I don't like it,' the poor man sobbed. 'It just reminds me of my wife. She always cooked cabbage. It was her signature dish. She used to add green food colouring to it, so it was very vibrant, nearly fluorescent.'

As Ethan finally composed himself and got ready to dig in, my dear husband suddenly leapt over and proceeded to cut our guest's meat into small pieces, all the while chatting as if nothing unusual was happening. We both sat watching, mesmerised, not sure what to do.

Suddenly realising what he was doing, Ivan laughed and said, 'Sorry about that, mate. I'm so used to cutting up Mansell's meat for him, it's automatic.'

Ethan, who by then must have thought he was on a

hidden-camera reality TV show, said, 'Oh, that's quite alright, Ivan, you're a great help.'

The cherry on top was when I started feeling light-headed and sweaty, and went into the bathroom to splash some water on my face. The next thing I knew, my husband was carrying me to our bedroom, with Ethan looking horrified in the background.

Ivan told me the next day that he and Ethan had had a very pleasant evening together – they'd opened another bottle of red wine and enjoyed the ice cream.

Maybe so, but I never dared invite Ethan for dinner again.

▲ ▲ ▲

Our neighbour Mick was a brilliant handyman. In his spare time he'd always be in his garage, tinkering with machines or building something.

One Saturday lunchtime, as per normal, Mick was in his garage with Danesh, a gardener whom many of us employed for yard maintenance. Danesh was a quiet, amicable Indian man, who went about his work in a calm and meticulous manner. He was always eager to learn new skills, so he would pitch up at Mick and Judy's house at 9 am every Saturday without fail, and wouldn't leave till way past 5. Mick would pay him for his assistance, and give him morning tea, lunch and afternoon tea.

Danesh and his wife had two adult children living in Australia – an amazing success story, considering the humble life they led. Mick was, for example, always amazed at how Danesh was intrigued by the simplest of things – things we take for granted and never think twice about. He was telling us how Danesh couldn't believe that a toaster could actually cook bread. They often had baked beans on toast for lunch and Danesh would regard it as some kind of magic.

'How do you do that?' he would ask.

'You just pop the bread in the toaster, and then you put the beans on top. Very simple,' Mick replied.

'Amazing,' said Danesh, almost reverently.

Mick was so touched by this that he went out and bought a toaster for his friend. 'There you go, mate. Enjoy!'

'Thank you so much, Bosso, most generous of you,' said the happy Danesh, looking like a kid on Christmas Day, his eyes shining with excitement as he clutched the toaster to his chest.

A few weeks after the gift of the toaster, Danesh arrived at Mick's looking anxious and stressed.

'Are you alright?' asked Mick, noticing his friend's unusual demeanour.

'Well, Bosso, actually, I am very not right.'

'Is there anything I can help you with?' asked Mick, concerned.

'Actually, it is the toaster, Bosso,' said Danesh. 'It is a most beautiful toaster, but it is not working any more.'

Mick, relieved it wasn't anything serious, said, 'It could be the cord. They often break but I can replace it. Do you have the toaster here with you? Let me have a look at it.'

Mick understood the problem the second he saw the state the toaster was in. Baked beans were burnt onto the heating elements. His first reaction was to berate the guy for being an idiot, but then he realised that the poor man had only done precisely what he,

Mick, had told him to do: 'You put the bread in the toaster and then you put the beans on top.'

Mick, a kind and generous person, said gently, 'Okay, mate, I don't think I explained things properly. Come inside and I'll show you how to make baked beans on toast. And I'll get you a new toaster.'

▲ ▲ ▲

Danesh was so grateful for all the help he was getting from Mick that he invited Mick and Judy over to his house for dinner. They were happy to finally meet his wife, Maira, but a little apprehensive about going to their home.

The modest little house was very basic, with brick walls and a corrugated-tin roof. But it had running water and electricity, and looked comfortable enough.

In the main room there was a table, four chairs and a television with a rabbit-ears antenna. But what surprised Judy and Mick was seeing the electric saw they'd given Danesh as a gift sitting on top of the television. It was on display, as if it was some home decor. They realised that it was there as the family's most prized possession, and that they were so proud of it that they felt it deserved to be on full display.

The table was covered with a variety of dishes, some of which they recognised, like samosas and pakoras, while others were new to them. Mick and Judy tried them all. Some were quite spicy but also very tasty.

Having eaten their fill with their host, Mick and Judy stood and were about to leave, when they were told that the goat curry was about to be served. They couldn't believe more food was coming and felt overwhelmed by the amount of work their hosts had put into making them feel welcome.

Judy told me later that the only thing she had trouble with was the fact that the wife hardly came into the lounge. She would bring the dishes and immediately retreat back to the kitchen. Judy and Mick knew she wouldn't be eating with them. Although they felt awkward, they also understood that this practice was a tradition in the male-dominant society of which Maira was part.

Judy and Mick were humbled by the generosity Danesh and his wife had shown them. They felt the same way we did about our experience of living in Fiji: joy and gratitude.

Melina and Mansell's big days

Every time Melina came with me to Tavua, we would visit Mr Singh's shop, not only because he knew us well by then, and always greeted us in his friendly way, but also because Melina loved browsing through the large supply of hair accessories, bangles and necklaces. Even his annoying sales assistant didn't tailgate us as closely any more.

One day, as we were browsing the jewellery counter, Mr Singh came over and, without preamble, said, 'I was wondering if your beautiful daughter would like to be a flower girl at my daughter's wedding? It would be such an honour for us if you were to accept. She will bring good luck to the marriage couple.'

I really didn't know what to say, and in fact I was already trying to look for an excuse to get my daughter out of it, as I thought she would be too scared to do it. But, to my disbelief, this little voice piped up in a confident way: 'Mum, please, can I? It would be amazing!'

'Are you sure you're up for this?' I whispered.

'Yes! It will be so much fun. I've never been a flower girl at a wedding before.'

'Your friend Nina is also going to be a flower girl,' Mr Singh said. I felt happier knowing that Melina would have someone she knew by her side.

The wedding turned out to be taking place the next weekend, and Mr Singh quickly went and fetched a little pink frilly dress, holding it up proudly for Melina and me to see. 'This is the dress I was thinking the girls could wear. Would you like to try it on?'

Melina's eye lit up. 'Mum, look how pretty it is! Where are the changerooms, sir?'

He directed her to the back of the store then came back to talk to me. 'Ma'am, everything she will wear is a gift from me,' he said.

'That's very kind, thank you.'

Melina joined us, looking beautiful in the pink dress, and with a huge smile on her face. 'Mum, look! It fits perfectly!'

'You look beautiful, my darling,' I said, admiring her.

'Yes, my dear, you look very pretty,' agreed Mr Singh. 'You will also get to wear a pink veil and lots of bangles up your arms. I also have some shoes picked out, if you would like to try them on for size?'

'Yes, please! I'm going to look like a real princess, won't I, Mum?'

Mr Singh told us there would be a rehearsal for the women that evening at the temple, and asked us to be there. And he invited the rest of our family to the ceremony.

That evening, June and Nina picked up Melina and me, and off we went to the temple. The sun set as we drove along, looking for the turnoff. The girls chatted excitedly in the back, while we kept an eye out for potential hazards on the dark road.

We arrived at a brightly lit building from which we could hear some chanting and loud Indian music. A few women were standing outside to welcome us. Our daughters disappeared around the corner of the temple, while we were instructed to remove our footwear and wash our feet before going inside.

We entered and joined a group of women sitting on the ground. June had told me to wear long sleeves, a long skirt or pants, and a scarf to cover my head. As I looked around me at all the other women who were similarly modestly covered, I was so grateful for her advice.

Our girls entered, and I was amazed at how relaxed they were. I don't think I could've managed what they were doing – each holding a tray full of flowers as they removed their shoes and washed their feet – quite the balancing act!

They were followed by the wedding procession, and they then moved to the front of the temple, where they deposited their trays and sat on the ground near the family members.

The rehearsal lasted about an hour, after which we were all ushered into the courtyard and offered a glass from a freshly milked cow. I'd never liked milk but now, being pregnant, I liked it even less; and I wasn't comfortable drinking it unpasteurised. Quietly, I pleaded with Melina, after she'd emptied her glass, to discreetly take mine and drink it too. The poor thing looked like she was about to throw up, but courageously managed to drink at least half.

▲ ▲ ▲

A Sikh wedding is a week-long affair of various festivities, although we were only to attend the main event on the Saturday. One of these rituals was the application of a paste of turmeric powder and mustard oil over the bride and groom, to enhance their natural glow. Another was called gana, when a red thread was tied to the bride's left hand and the groom's right hand, a sacred bond protecting them from bad omens. On another night, the bride would attend a mehndi ceremony where she'd get her hands and feet decorated in beautiful henna designs.

The big day finally arrived, and our girls got all dolled up in their frilly dresses, with their veils and bangles. We kissed the boys goodbye and headed off to the temple. The menfolk would arrive an hour later, and even then, we'd be separated from the men, not mixing until after the ceremony and the subsequent meal.

The place looked very different from our Thursday-night visit for the rehearsal. It was alive with people milling around, music blaring, and flowers and balloons adorning every pillar and post.

We found the bride sitting in a side room, looking absolutely gorgeous. She was wearing traditional red and white bangles as well as pure-gold earrings and noserings. She looked amazingly gracious and calm amid the tension building outside.

I'd been told that this was an arranged marriage, and I couldn't help wondering what was going through her mind at this precise moment. I smiled at her as our eyes met, and I hoped my look properly conveyed the message of respect and awe I felt for her.

A cacophony of car horns, loud cheers and music announced the arrival of the groom. The wedding car was just as festive as the venue, decorated with balloons, ribbons, tassels and a multitude of garlands of flowers in deep red and mustard colours. The men gathered around the groom and escorted him into the temple.

I tried to find a space near a wall to sit and rest my sore back – at seven months pregnant, sitting cross-legged on the floor for an extended period of time wasn't my idea of fun. But I quickly forgot my discomfort as I watched Melina and Nina enter the temple. My heart swelled with pride and love for my little girl as she led in the wedding procession. Nina and she walked to the canopy, where they deposited their trays and sat among the group in the front row, just as they'd rehearsed the week before.

The next hour was spent performing several rituals, culminating in the bride's pallu and groom's shawl being tied together in a symbol of unity, before they walked four times around the canopy. They then exchanged garlands and were pronounced married. The whole place erupted in chants and cheers, and ceremonial sweets were offered around.

We headed home a few hours later, after having enjoyed a beautiful wedding feast. Melina was exhausted but excited to share her experience with us. It was definitely the highlight of her life in Fiji.

▲ ▲ ▲

Everyone was looking forward to Mansell's kindergarten graduation ceremony except the star of the show himself. He didn't want to wear the grass skirt that was the traditional attire for the event, and was even less keen on the flower necklace.

The bride's red sari, made especially for her by a renowned tailor in India, was a startling contrast with her long black silky hair. The drapery was woven with a beautiful pattern made from gold thread.

*Melina and Nina lead in the wedding procession. Men and women
remained separate during the bridal ceremony.*

Melina tried her best to motivate him. 'Come on, Mansell. Everyone will be dressed the same way – your friends Tomasi and Marianna too.'

'I want to wear my shorts.'

'You'll have your shorts on, under the grass skirt.'

'I'm not a girl – I don't wear skirts.'

My poor little girl gave me an 'I give up' look.

Eventually, I managed to bribe Mansell with a new toy into wearing the special outfit, but it didn't mean he was happy about it.

On the big night, Miss Levatu greeted us in her usual friendly way, and directed Mansell towards the makeshift stage set up in the garden. The parents and siblings were sitting, eagerly waiting for the performance to start, cameras and video recorders ready to capture the moment. We tried to get Mansell's attention and make him smile by pulling funny faces but he wasn't in the mood. When Miss Levatu called his name, he gingerly walked up to her to receive his certificate, then retreated quickly back to his spot.

Once the kids all had their graduation certificates, a joyful song rang out from a boombox, and Miss Levatu encouraged the graduates to let loose and dance. Marianna turned to Mansell and started swaying her hips in the traditional circular, rhythmic hula-hoop motion. 'Show him how we islanders can dance, my girl!' shouted Susana, Marianna's mum.

Mansell, looking absolutely horrified, joined in with just the slightest quiver of his chicken legs. The contrast between the two dancing children was so adorable that the whole audience erupted in applause and cheers.

Mansell and Marianna graduate from kindergarten.

Mansell in his grass skirt, standing in the back row,
trying to hide behind the taller kids.

And baby makes five ...

My last few days in Vatukoula, before I flew to Brisbane to finally give birth to our little girl, were bittersweet, as I spent my time either sorting and packing, or organising the house, or crying about leaving Ivan, or highly stressed about the unknown. Finally, all four of us left home at 7 am, Ivan driving, to give ourselves plenty of time for unpredictables.

As we drove into Lautoka, Mansell shouted, 'Look! How many boxes does that man have?'

The delivery van in the lane next to us was jampacked with boxes in every available space; even the passenger seat was full of cartons. But what made it even more remarkable was that the driver himself was holding a box with one hand – an extra-large one, dangling on the outside of the van!

'Where there's a will, there's a way,' Ivan laughed.

Unfortunately, my next thought wiped the smile from my face. I suddenly remembered that to go to Australia as a French citizen, I needed both a tourist visa – which the kids and I had – and also a medical visa.

Seeing the blood draining from my face, Ivan inquired if I was alright, when I told him my concern, he went very quiet. That freaked me out even more, as normally he told me that I worried too much and that everything would be fine.

After giving it some thought, he turned to me with a very serious look and said, 'I think we've messed up. You're right, we should've asked for a medical visa.'

The rest of the drive to the airport was tense and quiet.

After checking in our luggage, as we were saying our goodbyes, Ivan hugged me and said, 'Call me if you get deported back to Fiji.'

The worst part was that he wasn't joking.

The kids spent the four-hour flight catching up on sleep, watching movies and munching on a few treats, while I kept playing over in my head my upcoming meeting with the Australian customs. I'd decided that the best approach was to be honest and explain that I hadn't thought about needing a medical visa. I'd tell them, too, that Ivan, an Australian citizen, would be joining me for the birth. I thought I could also make the point that we wouldn't be costing the Australian government any money, as we were self-financing the procedure.

By the time we landed in Brisbane, my head was pounding, my heart was leaping out of my chest and my hands were shaking. I kept it together in front of the kids, as they were nervous enough, with not having their dad with them. As we headed towards the customs desk, I tried to position the kids in front of me, as if they could hide my big belly.

When the officer finally looked up and beckoned us over, my legs were shaking. I handed over our three French passports and waited for the dreaded question, 'Where is your medical visa?' I had a flash of myself in handcuffs, being taken away, when I realised the officer was looking at me expectantly. He'd apparently asked me a question.

'I beg your pardon?' I said.

'I notice you're French. Do you understand English?' he repeated.

'Yes, I do, thank you for asking,' I said.

He nodded, tapped a few keys on his computer, then stamped our passports and handed them back. 'Welcome to Australia,' he said.

And just like that, we were in.

I quickly gathered our belongings, walked to the nearest chair and collapsed in a heap, letting the relief wash over me. After recovering, I eventually stood up, rubbing my belly and stretching my achy back, and grabbed the kids' hands. 'Our day is far from over,' I told them. 'We now have to collect our luggage and get a cab to our new home for the next few weeks.'

'Don't worry, Mummy,' said little Mansell. 'I'll get the luggage off the carousel.'

'That's very kind of you,' I said, smiling at the image of him trying to pull the suitcase off but instead landing on top of it and ending up going round and round on the conveyor belt.

A kindly gentleman helped us retrieve our belongings, and we headed off in search of a taxi. It took a good hour to get to our final destination, where the keys were, as promised, waiting for us under a pot plant.

All I wanted to do by then was put my feet up and call it a day, but within five minutes the kids had come running in to report various lacks. 'Mummy, the fridge is completely empty!' said a horrified Melina, and Mansell added, 'There's no toilet paper!'

We headed back out, not knowing where the nearest shop was, and walked for what seemed like hours. It was the height of summer, during the hottest time of the day, and we were all feeling tired, thirsty and grumpy. I was feeling completely overwhelmed by the situation: I was in a foreign country, eight and half months pregnant, with two little kids to take care of and no support around me.

It took a huge effort to push these 'poor me' thoughts out of my head, but I couldn't afford to crumble. I focused on the task at hand and directed my last bit of energy towards finding a solution. I approached a woman waiting at a bus stop, and she directed us to a convenience store, only a block away.

We were so relieved to be out of the scorching sun that we just stood in the freezer section of the store for a good five minutes to cool off. Then, grabbing the necessities, we headed off back down the road, each carrying a few bags.

That night, as I lay in bed reviewing the day we'd just had, I felt pretty proud of myself. It had been tough, mentally and physically, but I'd made it. I love the saying 'women are like tea bags – put them in hot water and you'll see how strong they are'. Damn right!

With ten days to go until the delivery, Ivan's mother, Eileen, flew across the country from Perth to help me out. My own parents couldn't be with me – my mum had just had a back operation and the long journey to get here was out of the question – and I desperately missed them, but we communicated frequently so they were up to date with all my news. And Eileen was wonderful company and a great help with the children.

It was so hot out that we spent most afternoons at the cinema, catching up on family movies: *Mouse Hunt*, *Home Alone 3*, and our unanimous favourite, *Flubber*, with good old Robin Williams.

The last few days flew by and Ivan finally arrived, to the delight of us all. The kids wouldn't let him out of their sight for even one minute. He heard all about our trip, the movies and the delicious food Nana had been cooking. At night he would cuddle me gently and stroke my stomach, telling our little girl how excited he was to soon hold her in his arms. Watching him made my heart melt.

On the morning of the big day, we all sat around the breakfast table, giving the kids last instructions and hugs, before Ivan and I headed off to the hospital. There, we were shown to my room, where I unpacked my little suitcase and got myself ready for the procedure. A few minutes later, the nurse came to fetch me.

I kissed Ivan and told him that I'd see him shortly, in the operating theatre. He was looking very pale and a lot more nervous than I was.

▲ ▲ ▲

Why on earth did I agree to this?! I thought to myself.

I was lying on the operating table, vomiting, as the surgeon sliced me open to extract my baby.

For my previous two C-sections, I'd been under general anaesthetic; that was just the preferred way in Europe in those days. But for this one, Dr Sandy had persuaded me to have an epidural. 'I hear your concerns about your scoliosis but you really don't need to worry about that. Nowadays an epidural is standard procedure, and the chances of anything going wrong are close to nil,' he'd told me confidently at our last appointment before D-day.

'I understand but why can't it be like my two previous births, where you put me to sleep, and when I wake up, I'm back in my room with my little baby in her crib next to me?'

'But don't you want to hold your baby the second she comes out of you?' Dr Sandy had asked. 'You'll get to witness her first breath. Also, and this is probably the best advantage of having an epidural, we can keep your stomach area anaesthetised for a day or two, giving your body time to heal and keeping you more comfortable.'

'That would be awesome – that's the part I'm dreading most,' I'd said.

'Okay, so we agree. It's a yes for the epidural?'

I'd nodded, then said quickly, 'Before you ask, I'm not going to be breastfeeding. Don't even try to convince me otherwise. It's non-negotiable.'

'That's entirely your decision, and I'm certainly not judging you in any way,' Dr Sandy had assured me.

I'd become sensitive to this matter as I'd endured a lot of mum-shaming in the preceding few weeks. I hadn't breastfed my other two – it had been seen as vulgar when I'd had Melina, and by the time I had Mansell, I was running the hotel and I couldn't envision myself on reception breastfeeding. It just didn't seem appropriate. But women could be vicious at times, and I'd heard it all, from 'Your child will be an idiot or a dwarf' to 'Are you scared your breasts will be deformed?'

I'd stood my ground, but now, in front of my doctor, I was

feeling exhausted. Seeing this in my face, he'd taken my hands and said, 'You're safe from any troubling remarks in this hospital.'

'Thank you,' I'd said, my eyes filling with tears.

But the epidural procedure had been, as I'd suspected, awful. The anaesthetist had had trouble placing the needle and had hit a nerve, making me yell out in pain. He'd had to pull everything out and start again.

This was how I'd found myself lying there, vomiting, while the doctor explained how he was about to get the baby out of me. It was a very strange sensation to feel someone pushing and pulling inside of me but with no pain. Then it all happened very quickly, with the doctor lifting the baby above the curtain separating him from Ivan and my head, and yelling, 'Congratulations! It's a beautiful baby girl!'

An hour or so later I was wheeled back into my room. Although I was still having bouts of vomiting, I was excited to finally, properly meet our little girl. But she wasn't in the room, and I started getting quite agitated, as no one would tell me where she – or Ivan – was. I felt trapped in the hospital bed, as I still couldn't feel anything below my waist, so there was no way for me to move.

Eventually, after what felt like an eternity, the paediatrician, Dr Marsh, came in.

'Where's my baby? I want to see her,' I said immediately.

'Please don't worry,' he said. 'Things are under control. She had a few problems breathing. She had some fluid on her lungs. It's quite common with Caesarean babies.'

'I've had two and never had any issues,' I said, very upset.

'She's in good hands. She's in an incubator, receiving extra oxygen. Everything should be resolved within a few hours ... or a day at most.'

'Can you please take me to her?' I begged him.

I was wheeled into the special room where I immediately spotted my angel. She looked so small in her incubator and my heart cried out to hold her. I could only insert a finger through a tiny hole and gently stroke her.

Ivan and I cried together. We knew she was in good hands and we were so grateful to my brother for convincing us to make this choice.

Dr Sandy came to check on me before leaving for the day and was very surprised to see that I was still without any sensation in my legs. 'I'm not happy about this situation,' he said. 'Let's remove the anaesthesia completely and manage your pain with oral meds.'

I hadn't really wanted the epidural, and I almost felt like saying, 'I told you so,' but just then Dr Marsh appeared with our little warrior in his arms.

'And here's the hairy monster,' he said, cheerfully. The name was very appropriate considering the huge amount of black hair she had, as well as the closest thing to a unibrow that I'd ever seen. But when he finally put her in my arms, all I saw was my beautiful, perfect little girl. Tears of joy started running down my face.

The door crashed open and my other two angels came running in, followed by Ivan and Eileen. Everyone got a turn holding the baby, and when she was in Eileen's arms, I was struck by the amazing family resemblance – they had same colouring, small features and round head. 'My goodness,' I said. 'I've given birth to my mother-in-law's twin!'

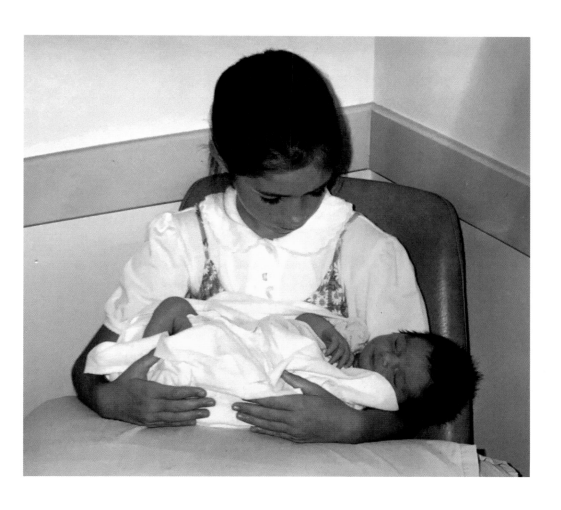

Our new little angel, Shanelle, in the arms of one of our other little angels, her big sister Melina.

'So what's her name?' Eileen asked.

'Shanelle Talei,' Ivan and I answered in unison. It had taken us seven solid months to come up with it. We'd finally both agreed on Shanelle, a pretty French name with a twist on the spelling, while Talei was Fijian for 'precious one'.

Mansell came over to me and, looking very serious, asked, 'Okay, now can I please get a little brother? It's not fair. I'm alone against two girls!'

On the move again

‘I got the job! We're moving to Australia!’

Ivan, with brand-new baby Shanelle sound asleep in his arms, delivered this astonishing news to me as he sat at the side of my hospital bed. His friend Tom had called him back in November, to say that a position would soon be opening up at the mine where he worked in Kalgoorlie, but we hadn't expected to hear anything more about it until the following month.

'I thought they were only getting back to us in February,' I said.

'I know. Terrible timing.'

'No kidding!' My head was spinning.

Three days later, Shanelle and I were released from the hospital. As we drove off, Ivan reminded me that we needed passport photos for Shanelle – she'd need her own identification document. Ivan had phoned the Australian embassy and been given precise instructions on how the photo had to be taken: the baby had to have her eyes open and there had to be no signs of anyone holding her up.

At the store, I sat on a chair nursing my aching lower belly, while Ivan and the photographer tried to choreograph Shanelle's perfect shot. The two men were ready, one with the camera, the other holding up the baby while trying as best he could to conceal the hand supporting her neck. But Shanelle was fast asleep and didn't look like she was wanting to wake up any time soon. Ivan tried tickling her, then gently prodding her, but nothing.

There was now a long queue of customers waiting to be served, and Ivan grudgingly let the poor photographer deal with a few other clients. Then, suddenly, it happened: she opened her eyes.

'Let's go! Bring the camera! Take the shot!' yelled Ivan.

But by the time the two men were back in position, Shanelle had gone back to sleep.

We finally returned to the flat without the photos, and Ivan called the passport office to explain how difficult the task of getting a shot of a four-day-old baby truly was, and was told that they accepted passport photos of babies with their eyes closed! Round two, with a different photographer and a shut-eyed baby, was somewhat easier to accomplish.

At only two and a half weeks old, Shanelle got the first stamp in her passport. She also was thrown straight into the downside of island life, with a mosquito-borne dengue-fever outbreak in Vatukoula meaning that she spent the rest of her time in Fiji indoors, and covered by a mosquito net.

Still, we were all happy to be home, although sad knowing we would be leaving for good in a month's time.

Judy had already left Fiji. She had gone to Sydney to comfort her daughter after a bad break-up; Mick was only staying on for another two months before joining his family.

This was a common fact in the mining world. People never stayed long in one place, and it was always heartbreaking to have to say goodbye. On the other hand, these friendships ran very deep and whenever you met up again, you just took up where you'd left off, no matter how much time had passed.

▲ ▲ ▲

The hardest part of any international move is bureaucracy and immigration laws. One night, as I was up feeding Shanelle, it suddenly dawned on me that Ivan might have forgotten to mention to his new employer the fact that Melina, Mansell and I weren't Australian citizens, as he was. They might have automatically assumed that we all were. The stress that I'd gone through because I hadn't had a medical visa the last time I went to Australia was still vivid in my memory, and I was determined to do things by the book this time.

I brought it up at breakfast the next morning and, sure enough, it had slipped his mind. He quickly got on to the Australian Embassy in Suva to reassure me that it wouldn't be a problem as we were married and had a child together, and that he had a job waiting for him in the country. But when he put the phone down, I could tell by the look on his face that things weren't going to be that easy.

He'd been told that Melina, Mansell and I would have to go back to France to file our immigration papers, and to expect a wait of nine months to a year to get our acceptance through. However, as little baby Shanelle was Australian, Ivan could take her with him straight away.

We were horrified and gutted by this news. He immediately

phoned the human-resources manager at North, his new employer, who put us on to their lawyers who specialised in immigration law. They concluded that we were a complex case but to hang tight as they searched for a satisfactory resolution.

After three stressful days and sleepless nights, the phone finally rang. They'd come up with a solution, slightly unconventional, as we had to enter Australia on tourist visas, and once in the country, apply for residency.

I could see Ivan breathe a huge sigh of relief, as he was happy with this solution, but it left me feeling like the kids and I were on the wrong side of the law, illegal immigrants of sorts.

While we were dealing with paperwork, I applied to the French embassy for Shanelle to be added on my passport. Within a week I received my new passport and felt a sense of security with Shanelle as a French citizen, just like me and her siblings.

▲ ▲ ▲

The movers came in March to pack up all our stuff, and the company provided some temporary furniture. It was like déjà vu, but thank goodness, we got a modern washing machine this time, not the old twin tub.

The container was packed, locked and sealed in front of us, and we waved it goodbye, the kids yelling, 'See you in Australia!'

That night, sitting among the unfamiliar furniture, I suddenly had another thought that made my heart sink. 'Ivan,' I said. 'I think we have a problem. You know how I have a new French passport because Shanelle was added to it?'

'Yes?'

'Well, I've just realised that my tourist visa for Australia is in my old passport, and that is in the shipping container.'

My super Ivan immediately sprang into action. He drove through the night to catch the truck carrying our container, then managed to convince the customs officers to break the seal and open it. Searching among all the boxes and furniture, he retrieved my old passport with the all-important visa in it.

When I saw him come in through the front door triumphantly brandishing the document, I jumped into his arms and we celebrated as if we'd just won the lottery.

▲ ▲ ▲

We spent our last few days saying goodbye to friends, co-workers and teachers. The hardest one to leave was Melita. But the upside was that she was keeping Shadow, as the two had become inseparable.

Early one sunny morning we all piled into our old, battered car and did the last drive down to Nadi, from where we'd catch our flight to Australia. We had a long journey ahead of us, with several flights before reaching our final destination of Kalgoorlie.

Melina and Mansell said goodbye to things along the way.

'Goodbye, bulumakau.'

'Goodbye, markets.'

'Goodbye, Tavua.'

'Goodbye, video store.'

My mind wandered to my dear Judy, who had predicted that

Ivan and I would end up in Kalgoorlie, like a rite of passage in the mining world.

I had the now all-too-familiar butterflies in my stomach about this next chapter in our lives, but as Ivan took my hand and gave me his confident smile, I knew that as long as we were all together, nothing else mattered.

Printed in Great Britain
by Amazon

73818442R00106